The Dust of

Everyday Life

The Dust of
Everyday Life

An Epic Poem

of the Pacific Northwest

JANA HARRIS

SASQUATCH BOOKS
SEATTLE

FOR MARJ & FRED, HELEN &
DAVE, OLD FRIENDS

Printed in the United States of America.
Distributed in Canada by Raincoast Books Ltd.
01 00 99 98 97   5 4 3 2 1

Parts of this book have appeared (sometimes in a slightly different form) in the follow-
ing: "Helen, Singing the Names of Wildflowers," "Little Helen Welch Muses on the
Fifteen-Hundred," and "Meat-Meat, Want Some" appeared in the *Ontario Review*;
"Midday, Too Hot for Chores," "Dot," and "Mrs. Bishop's Pilot Rock Chapeaux and
Notions Shop" appeared in *Ploughshares*; "First Planting, Gray Back Flat" appeared in
Paper Boat; "The Gospel According to Miss McAllister" and "Arriving with a Whole Scalp
Excepting the Hair, Which I Lost from Effects of the Scare Redskins Gave Me" appeared
in *The Connecticut River Review*; parts of Book Five and Book Six appeared in *Ms.
Magazine*; and parts of Book Six appeared in *American Poets Say Goodbye to the 20th
Century*, edited by Andrei Codrescu and Laura Rosenthal. "The Hardest Thing" appeared
in the program for the inauguration of Henry Bienen, President, Northwestern
University.

CREDITS:
Cover and interior design: Karen Schober
Cover illustration: Gayle Bard
Interior composition: Justine Matthies
Photograph of cover art: Richard Nicol

Library of Congress Cataloging in Publication Data
Harris, Jana.
          The dust of everyday life : an epic poem of the Pacific Northwest / by
Jana Harris.
          ISBN 1-57061-068-1
          1. Frontier and pioneer life—Northwest, Pacific—Poetry. I. Title.
          PS3558.A6462D87 1997
          811'.54—DC21   97-22943

Sasquatch Books
615 Second Avenue
Seattle, Washington 98104
(206) 467-4300
books@sasquatchbooks.com
http://www.sasquatchbooks.com

Sasquatch Books publishes high-quality adult nonfiction and children's books related to
the Northwest (Alaska to San Francisco). For more information about our titles, contact
us at the address above, or view our site on the World Wide Web.

Acknowledgments

I would like to thank Gary Luke, Kathy Ellingson, Robin Straus, and Irene Wanner for their help and encouragement, for their careful reading of the poem, and for their editorial comments. I am indebted to Alison Ashbaugh, Laura Jolley, Signe Hansen, Lisa Harris, and Marj Dente for their books and stories, and for access to their family archives. The Idaho State Historical Society deserves special recognition as well as my undying thanks.

Contents

Book One

LITTLE HELEN WELCH AND HER CIRCLE

(Oregon, 1865–1879)

I. HELEN, SINGING THE NAMES OF WILDFLOWERS

Umatilla Country, 1865

Blooming on the rooftop:
bachelor button, black-eyed
Susan, bitterroot petals pink
as taffy. At night by tallow dip,
"the spirit and the gifts were ours"
as we made up stories about worm
trails through bark walls next to our beds.
Our house? Cottonwood logs,
tules and sod above a dirt floor.
When snowmelt ran through
the ceiling, we children raced with
pots and kettle to catch the worst,
emptying in the rain barrel. Singing
and name games, rain games, then came
strings of packers freighting
to the Idaho mines.
Our ears pitched to the wind, waiting
"amid their flood of mortal ills."
I never tired of counting prairie
schooners, so tall I wondered how
drivers climbed into them — each hitched
to sixteen jennies guided by line jerk.
First came Hookey Burke, waving
a missing hand. His wagon trailed by forty
pick-and-shovel piled oxen. Next
Chinamen by the baker's dozen
getting the best of dust and mud,
a fifty-pound rice mat on either end

of their yokes. We tried to imitate,
carrying buckets attached
to a singletree braced
across our backs. Our favorite:
Whispering Thompson — heard for miles,
encouraging his team up a long pull.
We strained our ears to catch
contraband words. As he passed,
Mother pulled out
her leather-bound *Lute of Zion*:
"One little word shall fell him," we sang
to the accompaniment of spoon and kettle,
comb and paper, mortar and pestle, anything
to raise us up, up into
"A mighty fortress is our God . . ."
The power of song conquering summer
riffraff flooding over our country.

II. HELEN, MUSING ON THE FIFTEEN-HUNDRED

Father ran sheep. Wig-headed
and judge-faced,
they sometimes fell into pits, too
timid to bleat for dear life until
they heard Father's special voice
or Kip's bark. Papa always said
I would do well to emulate the traits
of lambs — submissive and close
to the sacred heart of Jesus. I darned
socks to the rhythm of cud chew, wondering
how the vacant-eyed
could be trusted to provide:
tallow, milk, mutton; wool — a dollar-
twenty a pound this year.

Winter on the Umatilla desert
so cold our Romneys could not
crack the snow crust. With my lost
brothers now only names and dates
scrawled in our tattered Bible,
Father hired bands of Minnesotans
to break through ice to bunch
grass so our bleaters could feed.

The hirelings! Never seen a stove,
their women cooked over open
fires. Not a match to their name,
they came to our place to borrow
coals when their mud hearths turned cold.
When 'Sotas spoke, they dragged
their "A's" over rocks, causing our sheep
to scatter as if stalked by wolves.
Father and Kip had to go into hip-
deep drifts, calling each back by name.
Later Papa preached: Flight
in the face of strangers
should not always be named
vice, whether it be
in daughters or sheep.

III. "Come Sit by My Side If You Love Me"

Odd how strings of words got
stuck inside my head — one, a line
of camp song first heard
on the trail west. The other,
my brothers' unspoken names,
heavy as the harnesses
our neighbor Yankee Jim

left on his team all winter
so the leather wouldn't freeze.
That song chiseled into my thoughts
like the names Father engraved
into two uneven halves
of a broken grindstone
planted on either side
of the rockrose growing
between barn and water trough,
blossoms the hue
of newborn lamb tongues.
I had to bend down
to read *Bucky* scratched
into granite on one side,
Chipper on the other.
Each time our neighbor
stopped to freshen Turk and
the rest of his team, he cast
a mournful eye at our rockery
and, afraid to ask, must have thought
them stillborns or tots
the harvestman snatched
from the tit. But
no child slept beneath
that broken millstone.
Lost on the Overland,
I couldn't even recall
my older brothers' faces, though
I'll never forget the song
Mother sang each day
to jagged snippets
of precious memory.

IV. MEAT-MEAT, WANT SOME

Wooding near our cabin,
Mrs. Joe brought kindling.
So old, she bent double and herself
looked like a stick.
Meat-meat, want some,
she told Father, who'd just been hunting.
Father said, for part of the doe, she could
tell us children stories. She knew
a little English and her withered hands
turned to wrens who helped her speak.

We wanted to know what it was like
when the white men came.

She'd been playing at Rock Creek, she said,
while her mother dug camas.
On the horizon, a string of strange clouds
pulled by giant deer with
buffalo horns. Women rode
on the white clouds, men walked alongside
holding black snakes which made
pop-pop noises across the animals' backs.

You'd never heard of white men? we asked.
Father gutted the doe and strung
it from a tree next to our outdoor kitchen.
The old woman's wren hands flew up, perching
beside her mouth. For a long time, she said,
we knew there were white men and white
women with animals called cows which gave
white milk which they drank.
We wanted to see this cow, we wanted
to taste this milk.

My sister Fiona asked, What happened after
you saw the land schooners?
Again the wrens flew up: Tyee† White Man
reached into a wagon, offering us
something round and awful and pale.
Scalped head, we thought, so scared
we could hardly run.
After that, Indians began following
the wagons. Afraid of white people,
they wanted to see what milk was like.
Sneaking up on emigrant camps,
they made war whoops, stampeding the cows.
After that, hundreds of white men
rose up like sagebrush.
A scalped head? My sister asked.
Head of cabbage, Mrs. Joe said.
Her man's name was Columbia Joe.
Out of respect we called her that.

Meat-meat, want some, she told Father.
More stories, we pleaded.
Mrs. Joe told us: Tyee White Man said,
the Indian needs work,
held out long poles to us.
At one end, sharp stickers like teeth.
Tyee White Man scratched
our ground with it, dropped seeds, scratched
our ground again. Plant, he said.
He gave us rakes and seeds and told us:
Plant, make grow, and eat.
We did not believe this.
Many times white men have fooled the Indian.

_____

(† *Tyee: Chinook jargon meaning chief, boss, or anything superior*)

We children giggled. Wasn't telling
a Siwash the wrong word for something
our favorite game? Father skinned the deer,
stretching the hide between two saplings.

Mrs. Joe's bird hands fluttered, swooping
to her sides, then rose again.
Once, she said, her brother saw
a white man carrying a bucket
of water the color and shape of the sun.
He gave a cayuse for that bucket, taking it home
where a teepee pole fell and broke it.
He took it to the tinner to mend
like a white man would, but the tinner
said he could not fix
a smashed pumpkin and called him stupid.
Mrs. Joe's hands fell from flight,
dangling on her bony arms.

She said to Father: Meat-meat, want some.
He gave her half the hind-
quarter and the hide.
As was the Siwash custom,
she left without
good-bye or thank you.
We liked her story. We wanted another.
Meat-meat, want some, we said.

V. MR. ELIJA WELCH, FIRST PLANTING

Gray Back Flat

North of Powder River,
north of the Grand Ronde,

antelope trail my only footpath.
Not a tree, not even a rock
for shade, the stone-strewn
ash-colored ground grit-
fine, rocks and soap weed
the same shade, lichens
the only gaiety — that yellowing
green of unripe lemons
scattered across hills rising
up to a coppery sky.
Sun the color of the new
plow blade pressed
down, pushed forward,
breaking in oak handles
to the curve of hands.

Midday meal taken in the stream-
cool of a canyon bottom
while contemplating:
A hundred and sixty acres waiting
since before Moses to be
taught to bear wheat.

Returning, startled two
salt-hungry antelope,
tongues caressing
plow handles.

VI. HELEN, BRINGING IN THE SHEAVES

We watched packers freighting
to the Boise mines across
a sage sea of dunes and
sand as gray as February. Mud

caked head-high on the barn wall,
my sleeves and skirt tattooed.
Hand-held, walk behind plow,
Father was first to break sod while
goad stick–wielding wagon drivers
ribboned our treeless horizon.
My sister and I tried to imagine
the miners' nuggets which
they sometimes brought to Mother
for safekeeping as there were no banks.
What if, by magic, our seed sacks
filled with gold dust? Unlike rock,
wheat nuggets turned to fruit,
was Father's stern reply.
He spread seed from a soiled tow sack hung
around his neck by harness strapping.
Eighty acres, handful by handful. Sometimes
I followed behind, barefoot, mud
jellied between my toes; now and again,
a stone to bruise my heel. When I looked
up, Father's head a shadow beneath
his hat, when he leaned over,
a sweat-stained sack where
his face ought to be. May, June,
knee-deep mud turned
to knee-deep dust, grain ripening
to nuggets. Father mined
the field with a scythe; Mother,
Fiona, and I following behind, binding
bundles the size of Baby Bessie.
Dried, carried to the barn, fed
to the fanning mill — like a colossal
coffee grinder — separating seed
from chaff which the blessed afternoon

breeze blew away, bringing the noise
of goad stick crack and packers calling,
"Something to eat? Something to eat?"

VII. THE HARDEST THING

Butter Creek Schoolhouse

From a sod floor beaten to hardpack
by use, we watched Miss Teacher sweep
loose grit, putting down
gunny bag carpet except for a square
near the stove for us to scratch
our letters and numbers into the ground.
During the first year, she
boarded at our house
as part of her pay. At night
we tried not to stare as Miss
Teacher climbed into bed
with all her clothes on,
changing under the covers.
We rode, three to a horse,
the four miles to school.

Neither blackboard nor books, only
tattered Bible and ancient almanac
to practice geography and spelling.
Our only light, the open door until
hollowed potatoes made perfect
candlesticks. Light or dark,
we mapped St. Paul's missionary journeys
compared with equal distances down
the road to home: If Columbia Gorge
was our Jordan, then

Mount Hood our Sinai and
— without question — Umatilla Landing
(with Spanish dance halls and
twelve liquor emporiums)
the Wilderness of Sin. But
when Miss Teacher made us hold
the scratching stick like a pen,
pretend to drip the ink,
now blot, blow dry
— that was the hardest thing.

VIII. WHILE FATHER DROVE SHEEP TO SUMMER PASTURE

Mama took in gold; twenty-dollar
pieces hidden in the hay
stack, parfleches of gilded dust tucked
into Baby Bessie's cradle.
Whispering Thompson and Hookey
Burke dropped off their pokes
pinching Fiona's cheek and
leaving a nugget for our trouble.
We'd no eggs to sell, and needed
a cow — sheep milk hard on baby's stomach.
"Better to have a packer or two
in our pocket," Mama said,
eyeing swarthy white men camped
near our cottonwoods — she more afraid
of Texans than Indians.
Thinking a Tex sneaking up
to our door, we got nervous.
Lifting the stove lid, we hid
Hookey Burke's six pokes down there.
This the only time I heard Mama

curse fate and mutter
my dead brothers' names.

The Texan had cut himself
with an ax, asked Mama to sew up
his arm. When he left, my sister and I swept
the floor better than ever,
taking filings down to the river
where we panned out a dollar
in gold flakes. Next morning
clouds rolled in; Mama forgot,
lit the firebox. We lost
about twenty-five dollars
in dust. For years we showed it off:
The old black stove glowing
saffron inside where a corner of
Hookey's life savings melted
against the firewall in the shape
of a gnarl-trunked tree like
the olives of Palestine.
On brittle nights we ponder it:
What omen this tree from which
no olive branch shall ever fall?

I can't remember when
someone scratched the names Bucky and
Chip between the "Y"
in the limbs.

Never worry the Blue Ruin
in the medicine chest and you will never
mistake pigweed for amaranth.
If you are blessed with a good laying hen,
you'll never go without
as poultry and eggs
can be swapped for most anything.
Though you were taught not
to take the Lord's name in vain,
it is fact, not theory, that you cannot
drive cattle without raw language.
When you see dust like a Kansas cyclone
and hear the queer sonorous thunder
of a stampede, remove the blue bottle
from your medicine chest
— the one you traded for six pullets —
and hide it behind the hominy
which you have covered with netting
for protection against flies.
Now is the best time for children
to take shelter in the springhouse.
Load your Winchester. A toothful
of Blue Ruin will curb your tongue
as you chase marauding cattle
from the garden.

A flat limestone rock is best
for keeping beef under brine, and lime-
stone improves the bones and teeth
of infants. When a trail-weary drover
looking for lost stock rides up full
of Blue Ruin, six-shooter flapping
on his hip as he eyes the ten gallons

of syrup you swapped for two
laying hens, then demands
you give his pony, Cleopatra,
all the Louisiana molasses she deserves;
lock the children in the barn
to contemplate past sins, re-check
the net covering your hominy,

and oblige him.

X. 1872: FOR HER TWELFTH BIRTHDAY, HELEN RECEIVES A GIFT OF A DIARY

Arriving home, discovered pigs
— Abe Lincoln & Mary Todd —
broke into our corncrib.
Held the lantern so Father
could repair slats.

All week: Snow deep as dust,
cold but dry, no wind, no school
on account of drifts.

Went to church.
Mother, Fiona, and I
pushed Baby Bessie's carriage
three miles, through axle grease
mud covered by three inches of snow.
On our way, passed Webb's
mired-down sleigh pulled by sable mules,
one with a collar of bells, *jing, jing*.
Mother said,
for every Goliath there is a David,
so christened Bessie's pram.

Little Peggy Webb played her organ,
the first in the county.

Monday, Tuesday: Sky the color of lead
pencils and school slates with chalk dust
clouds bearing down. Friday: Rocks and sand
piles so tranquil covered with snow.

Went to church.
Needles on the lone pine and branches
of cottonwoods beside the frozen river
encased in ice. Little Peggy Webb played
"Hallelujah for the Cross."
She got the organ as a bribe
to let the dentist pull one
of a double set of incisors
coming in like dog teeth.
Her father promised anything if
she'd let it be done.
Blessed are those who expect nothing,
Reverend preached.
When I said to Mother, imagine
having money for the dentist *and*
an organ; she said, Helen,
you haven't been listening.

Tuesday: School closed indefinitely by
Superintendent Missouri Tucker
on account of the new colored barber
whose two girls would attend.

Wednesday: So cold cider vinegar
froze, shattering the jug. Our house
no longer in danger of being

carried away by vermin — all fleas
and sand flies dead.

Thursday night: Made ice cream
out of snow and frozen
sheep's milk flavored with
corn syrup and coffee. Father
heard it at the blacksmith's shop:
a subscription school to be held
in the attic above jail.

Friday: Baby Bessie vaccinated
against smallpox, the sore draining.
Cutting teeth, her pain excessive.
Abe Lincoln savaged
one of Mary Todd's piglets.
Father intones:
Something must be done.

Went to church.
Little Peggy Webb played
"Rock of Ages."
With no school, she works
her father's hardware, selling buckets.
When Peggy hits a sour chord, she smiles like
a pearl necklace and all's forgiven —
Fiona always covers
her mouth when she grins.
Reverend sang, we all sang:
"Let the water and the blood . . ."
Baby fussed though Mother took her outside,
rubbing red willow bark
against red gums. At home
Bessie sucked fresh pork fat.

Never ask me whose.

February: First day of subscription school,
snow like goose down
on our thatched roof.
Fiona, present.
Little Peggy Webb, present.
'Sota Tom Hodgson,
George Bishop, Belle Bishop, present.
Below in the cells, Indians
howled, beating against adobe walls
so loudly roll call interrupted.
Outside, the wind muttered to frozen
sage and juniper.

Today: Our stovepipe caught
the roof thatch on fire, melting snow
and sod. Our plank cabin filled
with mud, and gunnysack rugs
had to be washed. Underfoot,
Bessie prattled in tongues.

Wednesday: One tawny spear of sun.
At school, Peggy Webb talked
about nothing but
the maroon and buckwheat roses
on her mother's new Belgian carpet,
the first in Pendleton;
inviting us to view it.
Fiona told her she'd have to take
the will for the deed,
as we were wanted at home
at railroad speed.

Went to church.

Tonight: Hungry Indians at our door.
Mother's neuralgia spread
to head and eyes. For dinner, a goose
so tough Fiona had to chop it
with raw turnips into salad. Baby,
her teeth like nippers, bit in fun.
Father ordered her whipped
to correct evidence of temper.

Saturday: Ice crust over snow glistens
under moonlight like sugared egg white.
Ghoulish coyote chorus sang me to
nightmares. Come dawn, Mary Todd and
piglets all accounted for under the house.

Went to church.

XI. MRS. WELCH'S GOOD ADVICE ON GARDENING

Horseradish thrives best
next to the new privy and gives
your necessary house a domestic touch.
Rhubarb pinks brightest planted
in the pit of the older sites. Neither
sheep nor roving bands of cattle
nibble either, though mad cows
in your kitchen garden will uproot
the hardiest plant. Sweet peas
climbing up the corncrib
lift your spirits on the longest
wash day. Always plant your
rockrose in full light. Two

little grave markers crouching
on either side will not seem
so desolate amid the sage.
When the blooms come full song,
their pale tones offset by
the hum of bees — that's
the best time to breathe
your midday prayers.

XII. MIDDAY. TOO HOT FOR CHORES.

Even sage hens were panting.
Belle Bishop and I dangled our feet
in a cooling bucket of well water while
sewing clothes for Bessie's cornhusk doll.
On the horizon, particles like a fine snow blew
across washboard sand and platinum
wheat grass. Sheep stampede, I said.
And Belle said, Corn silk
does not make good doll hair.
I told Belle wheat grass
would do better. Mother,
who always kept a keen eye on the heavens,
came out holding Baby Bessie.
Since my sister Fiona married
Whispering Bob Thompson
last month, Mama looked
thin as a pea vine, always wanting
a doorway to twine herself in.
I asked her, Who would I marry?
When Belle said, A 'Sota, I hit her.
Mama stared at the dust veiling
the sun, her face puckered like the apples
we made dolls from last March.

Every pot has his lid, she said, her last word
sliding into the hoof knock of an
Indian (was it?)
riding at terrible speed
for this heat. Mama grabbed us girls,
slammed the door, bracing
it with the chopping block. Pushing
Belle and me under her-'n'-Papa's bed,
she hid Baby in the pie safe, pulling
Father's Winchester from the wall.
In the underground dark Belle and I
splayed across a lumpy tow sack,
grainy particles grinding into
our knees, palms, scratching my cheek,
my tongue reaching to it. Outside
Yankee Jim shouted: White Owl's band!
Burned Pilot Rock and
heading this way! My tongue
clung to the sacking. Finally,
I'd found where Mama hid
the sugar.

XIII. WHAT BELLE BISHOP WRITES IN HELEN'S
DIARY WHILE THE HOUSE IS BARRICADED
AGAINST HOSTILE ATTACK

Helen does not tell you everything.
Point of fact: After school
my brother took her for a ride.
The horse carried double,
she behind. George promised
a short jog, but galloped
up and down Main until Helen's
starched dress flew and her hair

— living lizards and snakes.
Mrs. Welch called from
the butcher shop stoop that
she had a good mind to send
Helen to live with her sister.
Then we saw Stone Boy
— 'Sota Tom Hodgson —
walking alongside his mother
in front of the old calaboose
which is 8 by 8 feet
and has a stump for a floor.
Tom's mother seldom speaks
and has eyes frozen as carnelians.
George picked up a rock
from the newly graveled street,
betting Helen she couldn't
hit Tom Hodgson's backside.
Though a schoolmate, he was older,
taller and, like his mother,
never spoke. He tended his father's
sheep east of Pilot Rock,
not lucky like us living
on the Meadows near
Butter Creek.

Wagoning out to see
Fiona and Whispering Bob
we'd pass Tom camped off
Yellow Jacket Trail, piling
rocks in the shape of scrub pines,
in the shape of bears and
rearing coyotes. For shade?
Protection against wind?
As I mentioned, Dear Diary,

he was years older than us,
his top half broad as a beef
attached to cranefly legs.
We never asked.

So when we saw 'Sota Tom
and his mother walking past
the old calaboose, George bet Helen
five dollars she couldn't . . .
Helen gave a jump, tossed, striking
his shoulder, *ka-thunk*.
We don't know why Tom's mother
plummeted to the ground, but
when Helen saw what she'd done, she
ran and we ran with her. When
we got to my mother's hat shop,
Mama wanted to know what
the matter was. George said, Oh
nothing, just that
Helen and I had galloped
up Main and spooked
a 'Sota's horse and the horse
had pulled a shoe and could we have
five dollars to replace it?
Mother said, No.
Next day at school 'Sota Tom
asked Helen why she'd done that
and she said for five dollars which
she didn't get and the day after that
there was a fire-wagon red carnelian
wrapped in newsprint on her desk.

XIV. 6TH OF JULY INDIAN WAR, 1878
HELEN'S DIARY ENTRY

Butter Creek headwaters:
three herders killed. Wounded,
a sheep owner crawled
to the dusty road by starlight, wrote
a note impaled on a greasewood stick:
"Hit in the back, hiding in the brush."

Father, Uncle, and LaMar Bishop rode
the Yellow Jacket Trail
to Camas Prairie doing what they could
to keep the hostiles back.
Quitting their reservation,
Paiutes and Bannocks headed our way,
looking for recruits.
Sister Fiona and husband?
So scared they drove past our ranch
heading over bran-colored hills straight
for Fort Walla Walla. Auntie and two-day-old
Baby Gertrude taken to Bryers' Mill.
Built: one cottonwood stockade
fortified by flour sacks. Soon
diphtheria broke out though it wasn't
the season.

Near Willow Springs,
Auntie's husband saved LaMar whose
mount collapsed beneath him.
'Sota Tom Hodgson galloped
a racehorse to the fort
for military reinforcements. One

wounded herder left at a Birch Creek cabin
while Father, Uncle, and men took shelter
in a sheep shed. Bannocks, with horses
and faces painted black and red,
rode down-mountain full speed strung out
in a quarter-mile-long line, their right wing

encircling as they imitated the voices of wolves.
Saddleless, some without bridles, they rode
only with blanket pads woven from beargrass,
guns slung across naked backs. White Owl,
their leader, brandished a blade that caught
the sun's white light.

Ponies picketed, Paiutes crawled
up-gorge atop brick dust-
colored crags. The sheep shed
wasn't bulletproof, shots
haphazard. Father and the others arranged
themselves as if in a quadrille along

sides and end, poking rifles between poles.
LaMar: mortally shot, a second
(fifty caliber) ended his life. Where were the blue
hats and horses of the cavalry? Father
got hit, followed by a hiss of escaping air.
One lung punctured, surely he would die, but

he swore he would not and
the men's spirits recovered until
Paiutes began shooting horses,
our Old Jeb among them.
The shrieking of animals
as they accepted their wounds
cannot be described. Hungry,

Father and the others waited first
for the griddle-cake sun, then
for a muttony moon to set, and
hitched their wagon to what few
horses remained. Loading the wounded,
they headed west. For Father
every hoof tread meant torture—
galloping, out of the question.

At sunrise, red dust brought the blue
uniforms of U.S. troops.
Their guide had taken a shortcut
becoming bewildered and by nightfall
declared completely lost. Daybreak found
the captain one draw away
from where he'd begun . . .

Our wounded taken to Bryers' Mill,
fed and bedded, our dead
retrieved the next day. A sage fire
built over LaMar's heart, the white
bone-handled blade driven
through it well into
the bloodied ground.

XV. BOARDING AT BELLE'S, 1878

With Father laid up, we moved
to town. First the funerals,
then the hangings.
I don't know which was worse.
Belle says she still hears her father
snore at night. Mother kept muttering,
"My wash, whatever happened to my wash?"

Our school
was in the attic above jail
and so we played hooky,
and watched it all
from a crawl space above the cells.
White Owl, the tallest, palest
copperskin I'd ever seen,
was given time with his people
to say good-bye. Everyone
in town turned out
to witness the parting.
Later Mother and Mrs. Bishop
said that, despite their losses,
they took pity and sympathy
to the execution, feeling
redmen more sinned against
than sinners.

A stockade of fresh-peeled
cottonwood fenced the stone jail.
Aboriginals stood inside,
townsfolk in back of them.
Sheriff opened the double
iron doors and pushed White
Owl out on the cold
granite steps. He was bare-
foot and I wondered why
they did not provide him shoes.
The Indians formed a circle
around him, beginning
a dirge-like hum, swaying,
the ring of redmen dancing
as one, weeping but
without a sob. Sheriff
pulled a black sackcloth

over the condemned's head.
White Owl's friends took
his hand one by one, some
spoke, some sang, the drop
sprung. The minute Sheriff
cut the body down, White
Owl's young wife — she looked
to be about my age —
tried to blow breath
back into him, his head
in her lap. Tommy Hodgson
and I, Belle, George, and Peggy Webb
watched for a quarter hour
as she tried to save him.
Later, after teacher caught us
and made us pick our own
switch, holding our arms
above our heads, hands as if bound,
Belle said that even though
White Owl might have been
the one who killed her father,
she never wanted to see or hear
about another hanging again.
(She'd never gotten to say good-bye
before they nailed her papa's coffin shut,
and couldn't forgive the pallbearers.)
Something about the way
White Owl's limp legs danced
inside his pants and his hands
twitched made her throw up
well into the afternoon.

XVI. At the Old Courthouse Well

No one could account for the difference
in the taste of it. At dusk after
the hanging we walked there, singing
hymns. We left Father, who now could stand,
though not for long. When I dipped my face
in a bucket, it drowned the tannery smell and I
imagined the water tasted the way
a kiss might taste.
There was lawn and blue
jonquils blaring through the call
of magpies even in the night and
the companionship of Aunt Aura Riley
who ran the Pendleton Hotel.
She shook her cauliflower head and
Colonel Riley wagged his bootheel chin,
together conducting a chorus of: *If only*
sweet water were the only spirits
procurable other than harmless
homemade drinks, how many sorrows
would have never been?
I took another dipper full
and recalled George Bishop's breath,
the smell of freshly mown meadow hay.

XVII. The Kingdom of Water, 1879

The day Mama started talking
about sending me to Granite City, it rained.
It rained the next day.
The river rose into the millrace,
the town cows herded
to higher ground. As Mrs. Bishop

ran to move her hat shop
trimmings, Belle and I stood
at the window watching
men carry wives and children
like bedrolls, wet to their knees.
Father only able to take short walks,
bed to privy. The house stayed
dry until the minute water poured
in through the keyhole.
A Chinese wash shed floated past, then
freshly chopped wood, a barber pole.
Look, Belle pointed, an organ!
Peggy Webb's? It had to be.

Little Bessie's breathing rattled
the house. When Colonel Riley
brought her medicine, we saw his horse
go into a hole, even his gray hat
disappearing from view.
We moved upstairs,
crackers and eggs our mainstay.
A picture of teamster Yankee Jim and
his horse Turk floated by. I reached
out and grabbed it even though
Mama shouted for me
not to lean out that window
—*if you do I'll send you to live*
with your married sister. By now
I was numb to her threats.

A sack of flour floated by
looking like a dead swan and
that's what saved us,
because that flour

—which was caked outside—
inside made the best biscuits ever eaten.
Mother fell sick with sorry
for Bessie's misery and Father's wounds,
not to mention the typhoid water
this flood would surely bring.
We watched neighbors climb
out their windows
roosting in trees. Without a levee
the river rampaged through
our streets like a marauding drunkard.
When the waters dropped, Belle's brother
drilled a hole in the living room floor
to let the swelling down.
We scraped and raked and mopped.
It turned biting cold.
There was little fuel
and all of it wet. Mother said,
what a blessing I was to go
live with Fiona as soon as
the stage could get through.

Belle looked at me; I looked at Belle.
Get married, she said.
It's what men do when
they haven't digs come winter.

XVIII. Years Later, Belle Bishop
Recalls the High Water and Her Mother's
Chapeaux and Notions Shop

Stood across the dusty street from Sam's
Shade Tree Saloon. Once,
during a holdup, bullets

whizzed through the door past
the trimmer's chair where
Mama had sat not five minutes before.
That was the year of
the flood, when we had to pile
hat trimmings on high
shelves and escape with our lives
and Mama's wool dress.
"Count your blessings, Belle," Mama said,
pulling a cartwheel hat from lapping water.
"All your Kansas grandmother had
was a wilted sunbonnet
— they buried her in it."
Merry Widow hats, hats with tiny
crowns and short backs sticking out
a foot in front, hats no bigger than
the palm of your hand.
How could we save them all?
Mama instructed: "Belle,
always skewer your hat to the front
of your pompadour with a single pin;
anything more is excessive."
I could not swim and was not
allowed to play with the hair goods
Mama tried to save: switches, rats,
transformational braids.
The eleventh commandment:
Build up thy head size so thy hat
has somewhere to sit.
Mrs. Webb's headgear?
The size of a saucer with a sharply
turned edge, fashioned from blue
illusion, trimmed in forget-me-nots,
two ties knotted under the chin.

Dawn till dusk the day before
Mama had sewn its lining.
Her wagging arm reminded me
of Mrs. Brokenhorn's
fly-chasing tail, back and forth, back
and forth, stitching an ecstasy of
a black velvet bandeaux coyly
peeping through the brim.
Two entire days
to shirr enough chiffon and all of it
about to drown!
Hat shapes, hat stands, hat racks
threatened to float away while the noise
of rising water out-shouted
town gossip: The colonel's wife changed
trimmings so many times the straw wore out!
Mama put her hands to her temples
every time she thought of it.
A boat-shaped black velvet model
trimmed in willow plume and bird of paradise,
a tiny import covered with artificial thistle,
the newest New York headgear.
Mama standing there in her black
wool dress, paper lining
her leg-of-mutton sleeves;
so puffed up she had to turn sideways
to fit through our door.
I began to cry.
How would we save "Billy,"
our sewing machine?
Water in my shoes, my legs
shivered. With Papa in heaven,
and my brother thinking
of getting married and no

good to anyone, who
would come to carry us out?
And what about Mrs. Brokenhorn?
I asked Mama if cows could swim.
"Be good and be happy
you live in these times,"
she said, holding her skirt
above the waterline,
"when we have trimmed hats to
wash away the dust of everyday life."

Book Two

THE HOUSE OF BEFORE
THE RECOLLECTIONS OF THOMAS CORRIN HODGSON

(Isle of Man to Oregon, 1857–1865)

I. Precious Burden

My pioneer childhood?
Do I ever think of those days of hard
work, of sleeping on dirt
floors in windowless sod houses, back when
Mother made my britches out of cloth
she spun, knitted my socks nights while
Father cobbled our boots?

My life divides itself
into Before and After.

Of our ocean voyage, I have vague
memories of ice mountains and
floating elephants, one so large
I mistook it for the sky
while the blank sea looked
filled with wet wool.

When a storm came in,
Mother held my arm like
the dasher of her butter churn
— carved from Granddad's rosewood
red as sunrise — her fingers stamped
into the handle the same way
they pressed the flesh of my wrist.
She held me and
cried, never again to smell
that bramble's china pink bloom.

I wanted to eat the rum breath
of sailors on the foredeck.
The captain kept watch which is,
according to Father,
why we did not perish.

"Oh merciful God," he chanted, cursing
the vice of Catholics.

I was born,
according to family Bible,
Isle of Man, 1854,
to Charlotte and John, and
according to another entry
shown to me by my sister:
Mother a cottager, Father finding
better wages in lead mines than
shepherding before weak lung set in.
Another entry: Set sail May 8, 1857.

So cold near Newfoundland they feared
children would perish, and some did.
I took ill and would not get better.
My head and neck swelled,
my throat burst on both sides.
I remember Mother shaking me
like bedding and Father pleading:
Don't leave us, Thomas Corrin,
we're going where a cow costs
two pounds ten,
pastures a hundred miles long in
grass cow-belly high; where a man
can cut enough hay sun to sun
for one heifer's winter fodder.
Don't go, Tom, before I can
get you to a land where children
will never wear the dead
blue pallor of a lead miner.
Child — precious burden no true
parent can put down —

I'd sooner throw myself overboard
than your wee body.

II. 1857-1859: ILLINOIS, KANSAS, NEBRASKA

We tented even in winters
more savage than wolf snarl;
their ghoulish concert ringing
horizon to horizon. If I
had not been weeks at sea, I would
not believe so many thousands
of hectares of waving grass could be
as flat as God's table. At first,
Father tended sheep.
Our houses: cut sod and oiled canvas,
lumber a luxury. I learned to
whittle on slivers of kindling sticks.
When it rained, we stood
knee deep in mud. Shouting winds
worried our sheep. When it blew,
it rained dirt and those winds
never ceased. Bleaters sheltered
against our south wall, the bad-doers
brought in. Mother — not fond
of dim, foul-smelling ewes —
wore herself thin keeping clean.

We carried water from a spring
a furlong away, our path
snow-crusted. Sheep
drank there — cloven hooves
sharpening the ground to ice
daggers that skewered my
naked feet. At night

we never knew where we'd sleep—
passersby always made welcome.
Some bedded on the floor
laid out in rows with us children.
Men stayed outside until the ladies
rolled themselves in blankets,
then came in, undressed—
all woman-eyes turned to the wall.
It took I-don't-know-how-
many chickens to make a pillow.
We had no fowl and used
sugar sacks filled with wool
which rancored some
adverse to the smell. Mama
sewed by tallow dip, reciting
the story of Noah, then
Daniel in the Lion's Den, never
studying her stitches. Her hand
flew, not even a pattern, just an old shirt
like the one she replaced, her hand
like a finch in flight.

Riches when cowmen
(faces reddened by windburn and wet
from gathering storm-scattered cattle)
boarded for a night. Sheep droppings
made poor fuel, but cow kisses . . . some herds
left enough for weeks of stove light.
Coming indoors, visitors
took off their boots.
As wranglers slept
and Mother stitched, Father read
Revelations to men who rode
horses and were therefore unholy.

(Did God intend us to move
faster than an ox?) When Papa came
to the place in the Bible where
the china pink bud from Granddad's
rose had been pressed,
we recited from memory, gleefully
conjuring the cursed sea creature with:

seven heads and ten horns,
and upon his horns ten crowns,
and upon his heads the name of
blas-phem-y.

Then my brothers and I mixed up
the long line of boots, so not a single
pair fit its wearer. In the morning
the clamor woke us, and our boarders
never left without paying.

III. 1859: GALENA, ILLINOIS

Our spotted ram perished to wolves
and the frail hearts of lambs could not
withstand the knives of winter.
Near Apple River we had
a weathered board house with real
glass in one window and
a pitched iron roof. But even
the weeds in the road turned
a tarnished gray of the Galena Mine
where Father got on Sinker Tunnel's
second shift: fifteen hours
of dynamite vapors, shoveling
lead-bearing rock into carts,

then hauling into clear light
before fumes beat him
into unconsciousness.
Six bits a day, minus
our flour and sugar bill.
Mother traded sewing for milk,
but had to buy thread
as we no longer kept sheep.

Ours was last in an orchard
of two-room cottages. Our neighbor,
a carpenter, worked all night
making coffins —
his wife holding the lantern.
The hammer and saw and bright
wick kept me from sleep. But the carpenter
owned the cow, so no one
complained. Otherwise

it was heaven.
An iron bed with curlicues,
straw ticks to sleep on, and all
the potatoes we wanted just
for the digging, though I had to
weed and wanted to be grown,
as a man never kneeled
on hands and knees, woman
standing over, preaching: "Never
take what comes first
from the ground, Thomas, always
dig deeper for underpinnings —
in living as well as in weeding."

Mother loved her washboard and
copper boiler. She owned two
clothes irons, a neighbor
had four. Another had
a hollow iron filled
with coal, and it was rumored
the foreman's wife's flat iron ran
on kerosene. Woman chatter
made my head ache and I longed
to go to work with Papa, ride
down into the dark sure cave,
the small of my back leaning
into the lowering bucket,
the aroma of tobacco chaw,
whiskey, and a word
I did not know how to pen:
Minnesota.
What did it mean?

The coffin-maker owned a team
of bay standardbreds which
he drove to church, an act
Father thought scandalous.
Oxcart would get his family
to the Trinity safely with extra time
to contemplate. Horse and buggy?
A wreck a minute, loss of life
and limb, speed the devil's handiwork,
a gift from Beelzebub.
And don't you forget it.

At home I learned my letters
and tables — how to find Easter
and Moveable Feasts.

Mother's eyes glowed
the pale green of gooseberries
when she wrote to Grandmother
of wash day advantages,
my day's lesson to scribe
her epistle: "Thank God
for these blessings and how much
we enjoy our health now
that we have a wooden floor."
I wondered if she knew
the whispered word and began
to hold it sacred, my tongue
pushing its breathy pieces
from my mouth so that they hung
in front of me like a shield.
Minnesota.

Our floor wasn't
hardwood, but splintery.
As Mother approached confinement,
Sister and I pulled Papa's ragged drawers
onto our feet, dragged our soles,
scrubbing until, like everything else
in Galena, the floorboards
turned the ashy gray
of mental darkness.

IV.

As I watched Mother chop
the only onion she could find,
the word dangled from my lips.
I began to whittle pieces
of it — the dotted "i," the hardest.

Mustard plaster kept Father
lying down, but
when pulled from his chest,
black hairs came with it and
he did not rise up cured
as the doctor promised.
Minnesota, the word had not
betrayed or abandoned me — Father
fared better than most
when beams collapsed
and the wormhole shaft
crumbled over him, pumping
mud and bad air into his lungs where
cough syrup could not reach and nothing,
nothing would ever clear him out.
To one chopped onion, Mother
added sugar, vinegar, weighing it
down with a grinding stone,
dosing him like an ox
with the juice. All night the knell
of the hammer next door.
Not even the rod-and-staff
power of *Minnesota*
could drown out
the coffin-maker's decree.

V.

Late winter, I stayed
outside so as not to inhibit
Father's rest. On a frozen pond
the color and shape
of a goose in flight, I played
shinny with miners' sons.

We carved sticks from
maple branches, hitting
an ironwood disk
one end of Gander Lake
to the other. For skates
we twined sharpened wolf
jaws to our feet. Once, skating
backwards, I lost my bearings,
falling into the airhole we'd made
for fishing. Pulling me out,
friends rushed me home.
I was the terrible blue
of cold lead, breeches stiff
as caskets. Mother put me in bed
with Father to warm me,
rubbing my arms with
witch hazel. Father's face
had stubbled like gray
down poking out of the quilt.
Papa, I whispered, don't go
until I can get you to a land
where there are no lead mines.
Minnesota. Min-nes-ota. Amen.

This, all of this,
lives in the Before of my life.

VI.

According to Mother, summer
heat as hard to abide as poverty.
When Father went down
into the pit again, he couldn't breathe
and was prone to fainting.

Coughing took possession of him.
Minnesota,
shibboleth of every Manx miner.
By now even women spoke
the word.

VII. THE LIVING-CRUTCH BOYS

Le Sueur Country, Minnesota, 1860

When Father, I, and four
countrymen arrived, frost had killed
everything, except wire weed skirting
the peat bogs. Cutting it stole
the edge from our scythes, though it saved
our oxen when snow came.

We had one beef cow
which we killed and corned,
but not a potato and now no butter.
A barrel of flour, another of sugar,
some tea. None of us was clothed
as we ought to be. In December,
frog-eyed Mr. Kegg walked
to St. Paul, bought a whipsaw, carried it
home singing *When Orry the Dane
in Mannin did reign.* As planned,
Father and two others returned
to Galena for Mother — three of us
remaining. Out each morning through
ice atop poplars burned snuff-dry
by prairie fire, we staked land, cutting
logs for flooring. Soon our oxen grew
rawboned and could not be worked.

Carrying wood, the shoulder of my jacket
wore through. Midwinter,
Bill — our garrulous talker — fell silent.
Kegg suffered sieges of back pain.
Afflicted myself, I said nothing,
though not even ox liniment brought relief.
Rheumatiz, an old person's complaint,
a disgrace for a Manx boy to have it.
Mr. Kegg could no longer labor,
though his appetite grew
and his eyes bulged brighter. Bill, who
had lost interest in work, spoke only
to slur him. A lone book in our shanty,
Kegg's Bible, which I read and re-read,
memorizing the trials of Job.

One Sabbath, Bill screamed,
"Where's my razor?"
Immediately I trumped up business
out in the barn. While currying ox fur
thick as plowed ground, I imagined
a dead man on our cabin floor,
throat cut ear to ear or
a red-handed razor-wielding maniac
springing after me. At noon
Bill emerged. Clean shaven, he strode
across the prairie, never heard from again.

We began to husband our flour.
The meat was gone. Kegg and I hadn't
a cent. We went to Elbow Creek
for pike which I herded like sheep
over rapids as Kegg sat on a rock
and shot them. I was losing

the use of my limbs, and my bones
ached like bad teeth. Still,
I kept secret, though I stumbled and fell.
When fish got away, Kegg upbraided me:
What was wrong?
I rolled up pantaloons, showing legs
purple as mortification. Kegg swore
it was leprosy. We'd be outcasts,
suffering lingering deaths.

A month's time did not improve us.
We made minute pudding of our last
handful of flour, ate it, and decamped.
I thought Kegg left our cabin with
the faith of Job. Near dead
and penniless, I took courage
in his trust. (Later I discovered
he had harbored a gold piece
all winter, and my belief
took a good shaking.)
At the neighbor's we begged bed
in the barn and a bread heel
we could barely chew. Next day,
Kegg went on and
the neighbor lady kept me.

Mrs. Gill's hair had the comforting hue
of cinnamon. As there was no wood,
her two sons became crutches.
Half my age, they put my elbows
to their shoulders,
dragging my dead limbs behind.

One day a stranger came, his eyes
two stagnant rain barrels.
A surveyor, he said,
asking board for the night;
thirteen of us in a sheep shed.
The stranger noticed the clock
wasn't working and fixed it.
Mr. Gill became suspicious —
awfully clever for a lineman.
Mr. Gill believed that no working gent
should be without his bottle, and soon
he and the surveyor-*cum*-thief were tipsy.
When I hobbled in on living crutches,
the newcomer asked what ailed me.
A mystery, he was told, and was given
my history. He commanded me:
"Open your mouth."
"Teeth slack, gums swollen, breath
like a privy." He rolled up my sleeve:
"Land scurvy."
Mr. Gill cursed himself for not
recognizing my malady. Hadn't he seen
hundreds of cases in the goldfields?
Night came, I was sewn up in horseradish.
The boundaryman would not go to bed.
When the bottle was empty,
Mr. Gill demanded payment:
a dollar for board, another for drink, two
more for keeping us up until dawn.
When the surveyor refused, Mr. Gill
took the stranger's coat, saying
to pay or not get it back.
The lineman broke down, telling us
he was a deadbeat — once a doctor,
destroyed now by whiskey.

Before leaving he gave instructions.
For months, I lived
on raw potatoes without salt brought
by neighbors who would not
take a shilling. My growth stunted. I hadn't
complete use of my muscles for years.

Now, all persons mentioned
are grass. Mr. Gill died
at the Battle of Murfreesboro.
The living-crutch boys? Dead
of White Plague forty years ago. Yet
I thrived and never doubted I owed
my life to the persistence of Job,
the bounty of strangers, and
a tramp doctor with eyes
like stagnant rain barrels.

VIII.   MINNESOTA: BACK INTO THE HOUSE OF BEFORE

Locusts and debt had driven
our neighbors the Gills out of Kansas
where Indians ate grasshoppers and children.
Hoppers and Redmen, the dread
everyone waited for. Locusts appearing,
Mrs. Gill said,
like a vapor, eclipsing
day into dark, shelled bodies
falling like hail, breaking
branches of their precious
greengage plum,
crushing potato vines, the corn —
a field of skeletons. Crawled up your drawers.
Ate your hair, even fence rails.

You had to turn them out of your mattress
at night. Pigs and chickens feasted
on locusts who had eaten their feed.
Everything smelled of hopper: the well,
the butter, the creek, the slaughtered pig.
Papa, I asked, would we be eaten
by copperskins and grasshoppers here?

Inflamed with new zeal,
our farm became the pride of
our father's heart. Oh, but for an egg
to make cake, Mother said to Mrs. Gill.
We still had no fowl, but
ate prairie chicken.
I could not remember
the taste of cake.
Feeling indebted for my care,
Father signed a note for Mr. Gill's herd
using our land as collateral.

As we had no fences,
it was my job to tend grazing oxen.
Soon we had sheep. At first
only a few wild ones, horns
sharp as thorn thistles. But by spring
the sweet promise of more.
Sometimes if Bird and Bill foraged
near the creek (and if there were not
carrots, parsnips, and beets to scrub
the feathery roots from), I could fish,
my only pleasure. Sometimes,
I'd take Bird and Bill and
our sheep to graze near
the wild currants,

pick a lard pail or snuff tin full.
Once someone — an Indian, one
with an eagle feather in his hair
for every Chippewa killed? — stole
my berries and bucket. Work for nothing
was one thing, but the pail . . . We hadn't
many. Mother needed one for milking
and felt the loss of the lard bucket
more than I.

Stemming currants and tending cattle
and keeping sheep from harm
kept me from fishing.
Stemming caraway — nearly impossible.
So many seeds got away and one day,
our goat, the black-and-white bellwether,
ate everything. Then our sheep took
the opportunity to stray.
Limping along, my new boots
not yet broken in, looking for bleaters,
I came to a Cherokee summer camp
in a willow grove a mile down creek.

Ponies and dogs trumpeted
my approach. Men sat
on the pebbled ground, eating —
their faces streaked with redmite.
They were not unfriendly,
and seized the occasion
to boast of more Chippewa
slayings. One handed me
a necklace strung with —
I could not believe my eyes
and if I had not been

so afraid, would never
have accepted —
maggots like pearls.
An old woman bent thin as
a scrub oak plunged
the necklace into boiling water,
held it out for me like a skewer,
so that I could pull grubs
from the horsehair string
into my mouth.
She drew the thread away as if
I might steal it.
All I could think of was
I must say "thank you," and
were her hands clean?
I swallowed, did not dare
to chew. A bitter aftertaste
lived in my mouth for days.

My hosts claimed to have seen
none of my sheep.
I walked home. The after-flavor
took my mind from my feet
which ached. (We got new boots
in summer. Father made them.
Neither a left nor a right,
they looked like twin bateaux,
the tops more hide than leather.
Soaked in water they melded
to my feet, left and right exchanged
monthly so soles wore the same.)
Dragging my scurvy legs home,
a maggoty taste as biting
as magnesia bruised my mouth,

my new shoes gouging my toes.

All this time the lost sheep
lounged under the house.

IX.

Though snow could cut
and blind, I had to attend school.
I defended John Brown though I knew
not who he was nor what he'd done.
I learned to spell *Oregon*.
Only ten pupils, some boys
as tall as Mr. Saunders, who kept
a flask in one hand and a swatch
of birch quirts in the other.
Whacking them against his
thigh, he scolded,
"Much too much levity."
He said that if I thought
so much of myself, surely
I could spell *Oregon* backwards.
I could and I did and I whittled
it in script — though by this
time I'd discovered the kiss
of ink touching paper and prayed
the strength my legs lacked
could be found in words.

The log school had no light
or windows and when
the door had to be shut
it was too dark to see
sums on the slate or read

the numbers of Mr. Gill's herd
which perished in a drift.
The word *debt* walked off
my speller into my dreams.
School closed when we had to crawl
out the smoke hole due to snow.
It was the year Mr. Gill
and many others ran
to President Lincoln's aid,
while we were run off our farm
by his debt.

Oregon,
the word made me hang
my head in shame. With what
money was left, Father sold
Bird and Bill, cursed the vice
of Catholics, coffin-makers,
and bankers, purchased
a wagon and two mares, their manes
carbon, their flanks the pale color
of the last horse of the apocalypse.

Neither Mother nor I recognized
the man he'd become.

X. COMING INTO THE BLUES

For my eleventh birthday:
a six-gun.
That June of '65 my family walked our
one thousand head of sheep across the Blue
Mountains to Umatilla, taking only
necessities. At my belt: my six-shooter,

whittling knife, a cup. Between us,
one common spoon
for cooking and ten pounds of bacon
which soon ran rancid. We killed
birds and rabbits.
Every bullet had to count.
The sheep? Too precious to eat.
Trail grass dried to dust and we longed
for greens while the ewes browsed
on low hanging branches. At night
we slept standing up with our clothes on
to keep our stock from wolves
who carried off four. The wagon road
rutted deep enough to swallow sheep.
Coming along behind, lifting them out
was my job. Devoured by insects crossing
Mud Lake — so filled with roots and scrub
we were safe from sinking — we came
into the Blues, meeting two men who told us
about a hollow of wild squash some distance
off the trail. I walked six miles but
could not find it. Turning back, I saw
our horses trotting toward me,
their black, windblown manes just coming
into view over a ridge, appearing
as fire-scorched grass.
Running up a rise I saw the back of
a woman wearing an Indian shawl, rifle
over her shoulder. Nez Perce or Cayuse?
I could not read the markings on her mantle.
I aimed my six-shooter in case of trouble,
every bullet had to count, remember?
A miss would mean wasted
lead and powder, plus our horses

lost to stampede or redskins. I've forgotten
to mention: discord of any kind is enough
to worry the stoutest sheep to dyspepsia.
Left arm crossed under right wrist
to brace it, I took aim, began
to squeeze the trigger. Just then
the woman turned.
Mother
had followed, bringing
the horses, hoping to meet me.
Can I still see the tilt of her head, the hinge
of her hanging jaw, her hair
turning the color of saltpeter? Do I remember
the hard blue sky, the sun
a single white coal hazed in ash?
Can I feel the flexion of my finger
against the lever? Did I later recall
the Indian shawl she swapped with a Siwash
for a skillet of pancakes that morning? Do I still
see the horses' manes fluttering like singed
straw after a barn burning? Do I? Never
less than once a day all these
decades After.

Book Three

GRANITE
CORRESPONDENCE CONCERNING HELEN WELCH

(Oregon, 1879–1880)

I. Mrs. Robert Thompson
Granite City, Oregon, September 15, 1879

Dearest Mama,
  The dust
of everyday life
washed away when
I saw the gay
ridiculous headgear
Mrs. Bishop had given Helen
for her going away.
As the overland stage bobbed
into Granite, trailed by clouds
of powdered alkali,
Helen's rooster-feathered
three-cornered red felt
with picture-book bow
looked like a jeweled
crown amid its cargo
of unwashed bewhiskered
miners and Chinese.
Helen had her straight-as-a-candle
hair done up and looked
every bit the new schoolmarm.
Few white children here,
mostly half-breeds. My sister
(stunned to learn her duties in Granite)
said, over and over, that she
could not, did not know
how to teach even
a schooled child, let alone . . .
I quoted you, Mama:
Have faith and begin
at the beginning: Show

those who have shoes and
whose shoes have laces
how to tie them. She is glum
but settled, her belongings in
the little anteroom off
our warm kitchen.

Winter a poor time
to rustle work, we're
grateful Mr. Thompson
draws wages hauling to mines —
today a load of chickens.
Last night he brought in
one of a barrel of hams
which had been yesterday's
cargo. His drivers wait on me
like Maid Marian.
The doctor says I will be
sick in about five months'
time and hopeful that
by then I shall have shed
this cold which has
set up housekeeping
in my lungs. My hand
has the neuralgia today
and I've about worn out this pen.
Believe in my love for you,
Dearest Parents. Your eldest,
Fiona.

II. Miss Helen Welch
Granite City, September 25, 1879

Dear Mama,
      Tonight we had
a dinner of fried ham with
both bread and potatoes plus
Fiona's currant jelly,
so firm you could cut it
with a knife. If only Father
could have a taste — surely
it's the tonic he needs.
Sister and new husband
trying hard to find a cow and
it will be my duty to milk before
going to teach. Tomorrow
I inspect the schoolhouse
and woodpile. Rumor has it
there's a stove but no ax.
It's riches here and I can't see
what right I have to occupy
two beds, one in the lean-to
and one made up in the kitchen
for nights when the thermometer
falls below sea level. Be assured
that I intend to make you
proud of me. Your grown-up
daughter, H.W.

III. Miss Helen Welch
Granite City, September 25, 1879

Dear Belle,
　　Do not
let anyone see this letter
and do not believe
what my mother tells you
about my life here.
The fleas are my
tormentors. Large as birds, though
they do not roost in trees, but
fly from one of Mr. Thompson's
dogs to the other. My quarters
are where Piper and Monk
used to sleep before the cowshed
was built and on cold nights
we all share the kitchen floor.
For privacy I've raggedy
flags instead of curtains.
Tonight supped on ham so
tough it bent the knife.
At dinner, Mr. Thompson passed
me both fried bread and potatoes
which I preferred to meat
but did not know I was supposed
to choose between platters
and not sample each.
I will spare you even
a thumbnail sketch of
the lecture which ensued
concerning Mr. Thompson's
childhood deprivations.
The good news is

we have eggs, which means
we have cake when
Mr. Thompson allows it
most must be saved to
produce hens to sell, though
Fiona and I are promised
cloth for new shirtwaists
bought with egg money.

Was too tired last night
to continue, but
now can tell you that
the schoolhouse is
the original dugout
built when the first
prospector struck here.
My pay will be delayed
or come "in kind" due to
the frayed nerves of a tax
assessor who left Granite
unexpectedly. Some
good councilmen got him
drunk to stupor, laid him
in a spare coffin, covering
the box with candles, then
howled and stomped so loudly
around the casket that
he came to, running
for dear life.

I find most prospectors
rude and do not invite
their appraisals, though Fiona
assures Mr. Thompson that

I'm up to my old tricks again.
(Is brother George reading
over your shoulder?)
But why everyone
calls the Chinese lazy,
I cannot say. Tipped Soo Li
a dime when he carried my
trunk from the stage stop
to Fiona's threshold. He was near
bent in half, but ran
faster than Mr. Thompson's
dogs which nipped at his
rag-bound feet and tore his
black flapping trousers.
Fiona nearly crowned me,
saying a penny would have sufficed,
and still holds this error up
as not to be forgotten.

I mentioned chickens, but
now should say, there *were* hens.
Yesterday Mr. Thompson over-
turned his load of banty crates
on the stiff grade up to Red Boy Mine —
blaming an unreliable wheeler.
When Mr. T. discovered that
all fowl not slain escaped,
he christened that treeless knob
Chicken Hill.
So now, Fiona and I will
have to do without new dresses.
Believe me, Mr. Thompson does not
deprive himself of anything,
especially half a quart
before mid-forenoon.

I begin lessons next week,
teaching what?
There are not even slates, though
we have carpenter's chalk.
The girls I will instruct
in the making of cornhusk dolls.
And the boys? I have seven
days on which to ponder.
Mr. Thompson's associates
continually try to convince me
to quit the state of single
blessedness, a consideration
that will make me sit straight
as a hoe handle even
on the coldest morning.
Soo Li caught me blubbering
into the cauldron yesterday
when Fiona set me to making
soap to trade for a new hen.
Do you know, Belle, that China-
men call us whites barbarians?
When time permits, write
to your barbarian girlfriend,
Helen Welch.

IV. Miss Helen Welch
Granite City, October 7

Dear Diary,
    Never was a burg
so aptly named. Every
house made from the jailer's
own rock pile. Homes and

establishments set up anywhere,
making the town
cattywampus as to streets.
Located along a lizard-
colored ridge above
the white waters of
Onion Creek, so fearfully cold
trout flesh is solid
as a chopping block.
Some big cottonwoods,
some scrub pine, most fir
cut down for mill and hoist
house of the Red Boy Mine.
Gravel and tailings everywhere,
at night the races freeze up
and I awake to woodsmoke
mornings, fires thawing
the cleanings.

Many live in dugouts,
so I cannot complain
about our plank and batten
cottage with rock-walled barn.
Each afternoon, Fiona rakes
the pebbly yard, restoring
her stone-lined walkway.
Mr. Skedaddle Smith,
Fiona's husband's partner,
lives a few lots away
under an upturned tree;
a rooster usually perched
on the edge of his bean pot.
I have declared Mr. Smith
the dirtiest man living,

the front of his shirt
starched with tobacco juice.

Entrusting my sincerest thoughts
to your care, Helen Welch.

V. Miss Belle Bishop
Pendleton, Oregon, October 30, 1879

Dear Helen,
    George has no
one to show off for now
that you're gone.
He often talks about coming
to John Day River Country
as mining would surely
be more profitable than sheep,
but now that Father is gone
Mother cannot spare him and
walking there would wear
through his only pair of shoes.

Your parents, as you know,
returned to their homeplace,
now that your papa gets about
by cane. George and I
passed their farmstead
on our way to Pilot Rock
at branding time.
Your mother pines, I think,
she looks about
to enter confinement, and
Baby Bessie (who's almost seven

and shouldn't be called such)
pointed at me, saying, *Helen*.

Washing wool, a lighter task when
George and I had you and
your sister for company. I swear
most of the filthy sheepshear
floated down stream as I
beat it with a paddle, then
rinsed ankle and elbow deep
in creek cold. Much sheep
blight this year — George's job
to pull fleece from the dead.
It's as if illness stole the grease
from their wool and it rose
to heaven with each bleater's soul.
We are carding now. You remember
our mothers carded with teasels
when they were our age
—I am constantly reminded of this
and so pass it on . . .
Did I tell you that Mother
sold the mules and now
we have a team of light
horses and can get to church
a quarter of an hour faster?
On the way to Pilot Rock,
George and I tried hard
not to feed every oxcart our dust.
Oh, and by the way,
at sheep roundup
we saw Stone Boy
—'Sota Tom Hodgson — who
sends his regards and

won a prize for trimming
the most sheep in an hour
which, I think, tallied thirty.
There's no doubt he has
a way with bleaters. In
his grasp none struggled
as his shears flew across
back and stomach,
humming blades became
legs running.

Helen,
life in John Day Country
sounds like rough fare.
(Did Mr. Thompson really
cut the eye out of the king
of clubs with an ox whip
from twenty paces?) But
now you are "Teacher."
Think of it, only a few short
months ago the clamor of Indians
in their cells below our jailhouse
schoolroom filled our days
as did Mrs. May's
"Never mind their quarrels."

Cold here and we
wear shawls indoors.
Your letters make me laugh
as you are clever with a pen.
Do the bare granite ledges
behind your little mining town
really look as if they've
suffered smallpox?

Remember, dear Helen,
what Reverend Beggs preached
last meeting, *God closes one
door, but opens another.*
The river has risen and
fallen since I last wrote,
Belle.

VI. Miss Helen Welch
Granite City, Thanksgiving 1879

Dear Diary,
    God has opened
the gates of hell.
Last night I cooked dinner,
my first in this household:
ham (again), boiled potatoes,
my fluffiest biscuits, honey-n-
'lasses syrup over all.
I have never roasted meat,
only fried, and thought that
these stone hams would do
better oven-basted. Well,
I did not pay enough attention
to regulating temperature.
Black smoke poured from the oven,
the fire wagon came (I still
have a headache from its
terrible clang). I could not
stop coughing and my eyes
continue to itch.
The stone ham turned
to charred wood and smelled

like roasted cow kiss. The long
and the short of it:
dinner delayed and
the terrible stink of my culinary
accomplishments
crawled into our walls.
When we finally sat down,
Mr. Thompson refused to
bless our food as he would
not Grace "skunk meat."
Then after five minutes of
eating in silence, Mr. T. rose,
his stick-back chair upsetting
with such noise as to bring on
avalanche. He threw down his fork,
said, "You aggravate me,"
to no one in particular,
before quitting the premises.
That was yesterday.
Fiona is in tears still and
his dogs pine for him.

Today, sponged walls
with vinegar, twice scrubbed
the floor. The smell is
almost gone, though my
headache will not abate.
Doc Joe Young gave me
hydrate of cocaine
for my pinkeye.

As always, H.W.

VII. Mrs. Robert Thompson
Granite City, Thanksgiving 1879

Dear Mama,
    Helen cooked her first
baked dinner and today
scrubbed walls and floors.
My chest feels as if
I had two bricks for lungs.
Two bricks that bang
together when I cough.
This morning the sky turned
the color of ink, it rained
bucketfuls. Mr. Thompson
and his four-horse team mired down
beyond Disappointment Butte.
Six spread of oxen
dispatched to pull him out.
No doubt Father will say,
"I told you so," as he always
preferred oxen steadfastness
over the speedy but less
reliable horse. Helen is
making our house perfect
for Baby and I only wish
that mine could be raised
with my own wee brother
or sister — which is it? Perhaps
your riddle answered by
the day my letter arrives.
If only you could be here to
see my little family after
dinner when we gather
around the split log table;

me with my sewing basket,
Helen reading newspapers aloud,
and Mr. Thompson with his pipe.
He could be mired down for days
and we await his return
with almost as much hope as
we await your news — Love
and kisses, Fiona.

VIII. Miss Helen Welch
Granite City, November 29, 1879

Dear Belle,
    My students?
An odd lot. One mother,
who never had book learning,
comes to school
with her daughter. The elder's
penmanship unsatisfactory
because of misery
in the thimble finger.
The older boys
sit taller than I can, out-weigh
and out-age me.
Most are half-breeds.
Chinese do not attend,
due to fear of the proximity
of Mongolian males to white girls.
Today, dearest friend,
you must take
the will for the deed as I
am too tired to write —
chopped schoolhouse wood,

(with a borrowed ax which
I must pick up each morning
and return at dusk), tore
my only pair of gloves, got
a terrible splinter under
my fingernail, fed the stove's
insatiable appetite from nine until
three, carried buckets of water.
One boy with a large mole
right in the center of
his forehead hid the tin dipper.
Now I know why
Mrs. May kept hazelnut
switches in every corner
of the schoolroom. Daily
I threaten the boys with
floggings; to the girls
I promise knuckle-whacks with
the ferruled end of my pointer — I cannot
believe it is me, Helen Welch,
speaking! Oh Belle,
do not imagine I am unwell
or troubled with the fever
that is going around —
Your affectionate friend.

        IX. Miss Helen Welch
        Granite City, December 24

Dear Diary,
    This evening Fiona
and I and Mr. Thompson
sat down to supper and

Mr. Thompson ate his
entire meal with his eyes
closed so as not to look
upon females,
his orbs like bald
baby mice, verminous
but innocent. At table
I do not speak unless
spoken to, though
when Fiona begged her husband:
was there a midwife
nearer than Crane's Flat
and could she ask for credit
from the tinner
as we needed
a second laundry pot,
I counted fifty chews
before he began his
reply, intervals between
words the miles between
stage crossings
over the Powder River.
I have thought of moving
to a tent outside my schoolhouse,
but Fiona will need me
while she's confined
(where *will* I get the time?)
and warns that Mongolians are thick
as blackberries, though it is not
the Chinese who frighten me.

My secrets forever yours,
H. W.

X. Miss Helen Welch
Granite City, January 11, 1880

My Dear Mama and Papa,
    A new baby sister!
Your fourth daughter,
little Min with hair
colored the sunset
hour she entered this world.
Will her locks be curly or
straight? I should be so
jealous if she's got ringlets.
I had my mop tied up in rags
last night and this morning
it fell out like a spray
of crooked walking sticks.
I know Father had hoped
for a boy since losing
Chip and Bucky, but
you always said, Mama,
a healthy newborn is
all that counts.
And that you were less
sick than you expected
is blessed news. Fiona
is talking over my shoulder:
Amen to that, she says. And
——-she's speaking so fast
I can't get all this down —
that, like you, she's going to give
her baby nothing solid
until age six months.

Fiona does fret (she's gone
outside now to throw away
the pudding I scorched,
so I'm scribbling fast
as I don't want her to see this
addendum). Nightly she begs
my prayers for her and makes me
promise that if God, in his
infinite wisdom, takes her
to be with Him, that I will
love Baby and Husband
as the loss of her will
send Mr. Thompson
down the well of despair.
I placate her, but honestly,
since the kitchen fire, what was
a runny nose is
weighing like two
ballasts on her chest and
at night owls flee
the cottonwood outside
when she coughs.

Now here's Fiona with
the empty pot, dogs snapping
at her hem for more.
Did I mention that 'Sota
Tom Hodgson is here
working the mines?
I dare say he had more
color in his gold pan
than in his cheeks. He
looks sallow and spent
and came to Granite hoping

to get an apprenticeship
at a newspaper which flew
south just after his father
staked him to six months'
training and hasn't the heart
to write home about his
predicament. I do think
I will take him a rice pudding
tomorrow. Fiona and I
enclose a flannel shawl
for Min. Nightly,
we stitch baby clothes.
You would be proud
of me, Mama, I've knit
two little lavender sacks
with not one dropped stitch.
Kisses to everyone and
to our little Min from
your loving second daughter.

    XI. Miss Helen Welch
    Granite City, January 23

Dear Diary,
    My sister frets
herself into a perfect fever
when she should rest
to rid herself of the heaviness
in her lungs. I am to be
nursemaid as
Mr. Thompson pleads
exhaustion at day's end.

Last night,
when his fried corn mush
and ham didn't come fast
enough, I was threatened
with a strop made of
Bannock hide.

Fiona is short of breath, but
continues to weep:
what if she puts her love
for her unborn
and husband in front
of Him? Will God take
both from her?

Belle writes of George's
engagement to
Little Peggy Webb.
I wrote back that she
is more perturbed
than I could ever be
as it was me Belle imagined
would be her sister.
Fiona says she secretly
predicted it as Peggy
always did get her desire.
I wonder if they ever
fixed her organ after
it was ruined in the flood?
And who will play
on her wedding day?
I say it doesn't matter,
though maybe it does.
Truth be told, I have

had no time to think
of George here in Granite
other than to conclude
he was the kind of chap
to always say what
was on his mind, even when
it wasn't called for.
And if it's his fancy to wed
a girl who thinks "B.C."
means Before Crinoline,
then so be it.

Today at school
taught Bible geography —
Granite City surely
the Babylon of the West.
One of Mr. Thompson's
confederates gave Fiona
a Bannock scalp to make
doll hair from. She is
greatly cheered, but I
cannot bear to be
near the poor shrunken
tarantula and get a metallic
taste in my mouth whenever
it comes to mind. A bad
omen, I tell you, though
Fiona hopes I will make
a doll from it, one of my
best talents, she says.
I can't bear having it
in the house as it breeds
nightmares of the day
White Owl was hanged.

Did I mention that before
Fiona or I can cross
our threshold each morning,
Mr. Thompson checks
outside for moccasin tracks?

Skedaddle Smith bent
my ear (it's his ax
I borrow each morning)
about Mr. Thompson's son
(Dad Smith can prophesy
the unborn, it seems).
How the wee babe
will have a good-providing
father — doesn't Whispering Bob
wash the alkali from the eyes
and mouths of his oxen?
I would like to tell Mr. Smith
that if Bob Thompson were an ox,
I should not buy him;
pin eyes and puny ears never
foretold of a congenial beast.

My burden lightened in
inking these pages, H.W.

    XII. Miss Helen Welch
    Granite City, January 26

Dear Belle,
    Almost too tired
to lift pen to paper.
Today at school

taught acrostics —
it took my entire class
to accomplish just one
six-line "MOTHER" poem.
And, Belle, the rhythm and
rhyme did not fall
easily from cuff and mouth.
But their enthusiasm
carried me through as I
felt so spent I thought
my head would avalanche
off my neck.

Fiona will be sick
any day now and
I am thinking I will
ask 'Sota Tom
to take over my
teaching duties.
Believe in my sisterly
affection for you, H.W.

XIII. Miss Helen Welch
Granite City, February 5

Dear Mother and Father,
    I shall begin this letter
with the end and then
tell the whole story.
Fiona is now Mother
and you are Grandpa
and Grandma, and the wee one's
name is Roberta after

her father. Her looks
do not recommend her
as her nose is too flat,
but she has a healthy
set of bellows and eyes
clear as trout streams.

Tuesday night Fiona
became ill and the midwife
at Crane's Flat was sent for.
There was a dusting of snow
on Scar Mountain Road and
moonlight on white lit my way.
Mrs. Pitts could not catch
her horse and so rode
double on mine.

At dawn, no progress
had been made and
Fiona wailed without letup.
Mr. Thompson ran
to the Buck Head Saloon for Doc
Joe Young who was completely
indisposed. The only
other near physician
the Indian Agent
miles to the east or
the China Doctor
at Canyon City.
Mr. Thompson swore
no Chinaman would touch
his wife and baby son,
so galloped his fastest colt
twenty miles to the reservation.

The agent-physician gone
politicking for state legislature and,
according to his wife,
had probably passed
through Granite only
hours before. By this time
Fiona was pleading
for relief or death and
Mrs. Pitts and I turned
right scared. I wanted
to fetch the China Doctor
as he's had good results
with blood poisoning
when others gave up, but
Doc Ing Hay seldom leaves
his rock-walled, iron-shuttered
establishment. So went
to the saloon and, finding
Doc Joe Young slightly improved,
brewed him coffee and
fed milk toast. What he
craved was poached chicken,
so ordered my only pullet's
neck wrung and
within an hour fragrance
of fricassee filled the alehouse.
Doc Young became indescribably
ill and I gave up in disgust.
By now sweat poured
from Fiona's brow and
she panted in the shallow
quick breaths of
a dying horse.
"Thank God," I said aloud

when Mr. Thompson came though
the door with the Indian Agent,
who had to have supper
before he'd begin.

By now
it was the wee hours
of the following morning and
the government doctor took
half an hour to wash,
eat fricassee, then wash again.
Reaching into his bag for
the chloroform bottle,
he claimed to have saved
a hundred cases like Fiona's.
Only then did he discover
the sedative missing.
"Run to Doc Young's
for supplies," he commanded.
I asked if Fiona would last,
I'd never seen anything living
as white as her face.
"Can't work on her
without chloroform," he said,
"she'll fuss." I awoke
Mrs. Young who had to dress
before she hunted Doc's drugs
which she'd never before had
anything to do with.
Almost first light before
I got back, Fiona so
exhausted she could scarcely
roll her eyes. Mrs. Pitts took
a fit of weeping, then

Mr. Thompson
succumbed to nervous
prostration on the floor,
now and then beating
his head with his fists.
Not even his dogs
could console him.

I held a chloroformed rag
to Fiona's face each time she
raised her hand to heaven and when
her arm dropped limply,
drew the rag away as
the Indian Agent saved
her and Baby Roberta.

Fiona sleeps now,
and only in minor pain,
her brow too cool
to foretell a fever.
She barely awakens
to Baby's bawling, though
sometimes her own coughing
startles her from deepest
slumber. Mr. Thompson
says to send his best and
remarks that Baby's looks
mean little to him. We send
our united love, Your newest
Auntie Helen.

XIV. H.W.
Granite City, February 5

Dear Diary,
    Fiona forbids me
to write this news to anyone:
The day before Berta arrived
our house burned down, none
can say exactly how.
Skedaddle Smith,
who can stretch the truth
farther than any man, swears
the credit isn't his, though
I saw him, overcoat pockets
filled with inkwells,
begging passersby to toss
them into the air for him
to shoot at — most showing
evidence of black powder.
The thatch of our roof
caught first . . . The long and
the short of it: We now live
in the barn which, being stone,
did not burn. It is better
insulated once the stove's
cranked up, but cannot
be made toasty as a house
on account of the health
of Mr. Thompson's prize
stallion and band of mares.
Dear Diary, I never knew
how horses snored at night,
perpetually striking iron-
rimmed hoofs at stall walls

for want of feed, incessantly
rubbing rumps against the door.
I'm so fatigued from sleeplessness
with no hope of relief — worse,
Mr. Thompson absents himself
without explanation more and
more often. Your Somnambulant, H. W.

XV. Mrs. Robert Thompson
Granite City, February 21

Dear Mama and Papa,
    I am only allowed
to sit up for a few minutes
at a time, so Helen pens
this letter to say I am
regaining strength slowly
and should soon be able to
get back to my kitchen. I am
in precious little pain, though
what ails me is that
my husband has been mired
down on the road to Brownsville
for a week now
and cannot see how his
biscuit baby girl
fills my lap. She has Helen's
dark straight hair,
no measure of my curl.
Her little hands and feet,
pink seashells, and her eyes,
the blue of chinaberries.

Dearest Parents,
I was so terribly sick,
near the end regretting
husband and marriage, and would
have gladly gone to my reward.
Thinking of your hardships, Mama,
kept me during my trial.
I recalled earliest childhood —
how old was I, maybe four,
when we left Ohio? I recalled
Helen just a bundle as my
brothers' freckled faces
fleshed out in front of me;
Chipper before he took the cholera
at Money Creek and Bucky —
I'd forgotten Bucky had
a cleft chin, a chipped
front tooth. Mother,
in my dreams I saw again
the mule Bucky rode,
old Figure 4,
blaze broad and white
as a bedsheet,
saw the way his nostrils flared
when he spooked at
we-never-knew-what, stampeding
across the Snake.
A good swimmer, that pack animal,
Father assured, but
something was wrong,
the mule sank like a frying pan.
The pack saddle's foregirth
broken, our mule's hind legs
caught in the aftercinch.

We held over for a day
looking for mule and rider.
I remember Helen couldn't
sleep when the wagon stopped
moving (and later when we got
to Pendleton, couldn't nap
inside a house as clock tick
confounded her). The pack saddle
washed up a mile downstream, but
mule and boy were never found.
He is alive still, Mother,
I know it. What came to me
in my agony was that near-
drowning damaged his ears,
and so Bucky could not hear
questions put to him when
picked up by mountainmen
or wagonmaster. Did he even
know Father's full name or
place of birth? It's been nearly
twenty years, but he's
out there, Mama. Even Helen
says my trials have rendered
me second sight . . .

Baby cries,
and Helen threatens to
take away pen and ink
as I've worked myself into
a fever, my strength
falling out from under me
like carpet atop a mud-
flooded floor. 'Sota Tom
has taken over Helen's

schoolhouse duties and
comes daily to help haul
water for Baby's bath.
I now bear burdens
never felt before, and
Little One does tire my
arms as she cries and
cries to be held, but
her talking eyes make
it all worthwhile.
Kisses and Love,
Fiona Welch Thompson.

XVI. H.W.
Granite City, March 10

Dear Diary,
    I cannot keep
a single thought in my head.
Fiona is alternately
elated or sinking and
not permitted out of bed.
From the barn door,
I keep vigil on the street,
the stage road, my eye
nailed up where
two wagon ruts hinge
into the horizon, praying
for Whispering Thompson.

Can you imagine I'd ever
be so desperate?
As a child I strained

my ear across sage and saltwort
hoping to hear him
urging his team on with
blasphemies. Here I am,
still waiting for his hoof
knock and goad crack.

Little Berta sleeps but few
hours and am run off my feet
with fatigue or worry.
'Sota Tom helps me
lift Fiona out of bed,
together we walk her
to the outhouse. Once when
he startled Fiona awake,
she thought he was
our lost brother Chipper.
"What's happened to your
legs, Chip?" she asked.
"They're thin as canes."
'Sota must have suffered
greatly from the scurvy, though
he is better at his letters
than I and so teaches well.
He wrote home that he was
now *Professor Hodgson*,
which made me laugh.
Tom hopes to save from his
twenty-five a month to buy
another printer's apprenticeship.

Baby Berta, fat butter lump,
tests her lungs hourly.
Fiona can only hold down

rice gruel which cannot be
nutritious enough for Bertie, though
she fattens like a suckling pig
while Fiona grows frail as
a spider web. Am much too
distracted to knit, though
we need new socks, and
washing has turned my hands
the raw color of crawfish claws.
Nightly I bind them up swabbed
in the same remedy which brings
cow udders relief.

March truly
the meanest month. Lighter
early and late, but so cold
I've chilblains on my
lower legs and the wind
crying in the canyon is
sharper than dog bite.
The thatch has blown
off our roof, in places
holes big enough
to throw a cat through.
Miners imbibing
at the Buck Head
surly as coyotes
for want of work
and fair weather.
Few trout bite and
most sourdoughs spend gray
after gray day in their
rock cabins, pressing powder
into plugs. Their dawn-to-dusk

hours spent picking off
prairie dogs infected
with mange caught from
eating Indian ponies
that died of same.
The Bannock horses
have nowhere
to graze, their habitat
stolen by cattlemen,
and so fall to ill health
and varmints.
The sight and smell
of a hairless shivering
mite-blighted cayuse
begging food at my door
hurls me into despair.
Where is Mr. Thompson?!
Fiona needs more of a cure
than Doc Joe Young's
milk of magnesia purges,
and living in a barn
has frayed our nerves to rags.
As my pen puts a tail
on that last "s,"
Baby Bertie wails and
a sick cayuse eats
cow kisses intended
for our stove.

March mud never so treacherous,
Mr. Thompson never absent so long.
I remain as ever, your faithful Helen.

XVII. Miss Helen Welch
Canyon City, Oregon, April 6, 1880

Dear Belle,
    So many weeks
since I've written
with much to tell. I would
be a liar to say we're leisurely
tenting on the John Day
as we're holed up
in a dugout *cum* cave.
You remember that
China Doctor whom Soo Li
told me about?
Tom Hodgson
borrowed a wagon and
brought us to him
in Tiger Town
a short distance from
our new sod-walled digs.

Fiona had begun to fail more
each day and Mr. Thompson
returned only to leave
for Camas Prairie pleading
emergency with one of his teams.
Tom said, "Something must be done."
Fiona needed warmer quarters,
constant doctoring.
Skedaddle Smith, who was there
at the time, told me of this dugout,
muttering about Mr. T.'s *other family*
— news to me, I'd thought him orphaned.

A hard field to till,
but finally Fiona
can raise herself up.
When treatment first began,
Doc Ing Hay's boiling brew
smelled poisonous and tasted
worse, staining Fiona's teeth
browngreen. Now
mother and child would either
sink or swim — Lord strike me
dead to wish it, but
I could not go on
in such exhaustion,
ready to give up and
die with them if that be
God's plan.

A Chinaman
dressed in black woolly chaps
and white Stetson
drove Doc Hay to our camp,
where Thomas had replastered
our dugout, setting up
stove and rain barrel — as a boy
on the prairie he'd learned
the language of sod,
his handiwork keeping us
from wind, river chill, and mice.

"American barbarian matron
and infant," said the China Doctor
in a mingled tongue — hard to
understand 'til I got used to
verb-nouns, noun-verbs,

articles and conjunctions avoided
as if they were fatal.

Ing Hay had a feather touch,
softer than the tip
of the queue running
down his back.
Fiona's pulse, he said,
felt like a stone thrown
into a flooding creek.
He took nine-times-three
readings to discover what
source her disharmonious state—
a name for which there was
no barbarian translation.
The China cowboy,
Doc Hay's assistant,
spoke good English,
handled the horses
and mixed herbs
as prescribed:
yellow hemp, rhubarb,
bitter-seeded Persian bean,
extract of papaverine,
extract of ginseng.

Daily the China Doctor ran
a coin along Fiona's spine,
painted ointment
on her chest, blew
red dust over the white
tablecloth of her tongue.
Then for a week
compelled her

to suck prune lozenges
tasting of alum.

When Fiona improved,
we began walking from
Canyon City to Tiger Town
to his storefront, a fieldstone
trading post, windows
shuttered in sheet iron.
Belle, it's like nothing
I've ever seen. Dim inside,
the heavy dark of rock
houses, air thick with
a sweet smoke that,
when I cough,
makes my throat feel
as if I'm drinking
hard cider.

Patients come for daily doses,
as does the banker
who favors fan-tan.
Thomas buys tobacco
there which he barters
for food in Granite.
The inside wallpapered in
crazy calendars and filled
with music played on a queer
two-stringed guitar. Behind
Doc Hay's herb concession,
a shrine where a tiny
stone god sits inside
a brick oven next to
a smudge pot and offerings

of grapefruit. Once,
I saw Doc converse
with the baby god by
means of divining sticks.

To the grotto's right,
I know not what,
but white and Asian
alike pass between two
red tine-tongued dragons
painted on burlap curtains into
muted conversation,
fey laughter, and pipe smoke.

Believe always in
my friendship for you,
Helen.

XVIII. H.W.
Canyon City, May 18

Dear Diary,
    Have begun
taking in scholars

Tom, Tom the piper's son

That rhyme carved into
the wall of my schoolhouse
back in Granite. Now
I can't get Thomas Hodgson
out of my head.

stole a pig, and away he run

Sometimes
it's like nits in my hair,
the more I scratch
the more they itch.

Help me to keep my mind
on the task at hand,
— my nightly prayer.

Daily I thank God
for Mother's good advice.
If I had not had her example

the pig was eat
and Tom was beat
and Tom ran crying down the street

Fiona and I might have
starved here.
When we arrived
our campsite strewn with bones —
the previous tenants
jerked deer for miners.
As I boiled ribs for what
fat could be found,
I again thanked Providence:
government cattle pens nearby
supply fuel as all scrub pine
cut except for a ring
up near timberline.

Tom, Tom the shepherd's son
walks on stilts and cannot run

The river only a few
hundred feet below us,
I don't have to
spend all morning
hauling water to
leach wood ash while
checking scholars' slates
— spelling, penmanship,
punctuation — finally cooking
fat and lye to
the consistency
of oatmeal.

His dam was deaf,
his sire was dumb

Scholars and skewed rhymes, yes,
but soap has become our mainstay.
And I am never for want
of bones to render as
stockman supply wagonfuls.

Once
at the China Trading Post,
Doc Hay gave me
a vial of rose essence,
so scented the soap
which I first made to
clean Baby, but then
cut into cream cakes
selling to cattlemen,
prospectors, even Ing Hay.

Little Tommy Tucker
sang for his supper

Compensated in coin and gold dust,

What shall he eat?
—white bread and butter

some extended with sand,
but never mind — it pays
for Fiona's treatments,
food staples, and, best of all,
buys me pullets who soon
lay or go to stew pots.
So we are well fed
(when I can borrow space
in an oven in town, there's cake!).

Bertie the fattest corn fritter
you can imagine, though her
nose perpetually runs. Our best
laying hens kept caged
in the cave under our bed;

Little Tommy Tittlemouse
lived in a little house

all fowl brought in at night,
their perfume driving us out
onto our "porch" each morning.
"If you have hens, you can trade
eggs for most anything,"
Fiona quotes Mother often.

Fiona to return
to Pendleton as soon as
she and Berta have the stamina

for travel. Mama's Little Min
to have a same-age niece
for a sister. Mr. Thompson

Helen's tears and Tommy's fears
will make them old before their years

cannot be found, though many
here know of him.
Horsethief Campbell, a man
weighing 300 potato-sack-pounds
who rides an immense potato-colored horse,
said Whispering Bob's grown son
the spitting image of him.
I don't think Mr. T.'s parents are

Diddle diddle dumple, my son Tom
Went to bed with his breeches on

the "other family" spoken of
with bated breath in Granite, but
have mentioned nothing of
duplicity
to Fiona who waits
for her husband with
the faith of a seaman's widow.

Daily, except for the Sabbath,
I make soap and
tend chickens and
rehearse pupils in
arithmetic tables.
The youngest rocks Bertie's
cradle which Tom Hodgson

whittled from a driftwood stump,
the eldest wets her whistle
every hour.
The little boys tell me
they're tired of
Tom Tom jingles
and couldn't they have
a Peter Pumpkin or
a Georgie Porgie or even
a Going to St. Ives —
seven men with seven
wives each with seven
sacks and in them seven
cats and for each cat seven
kits — even the vexation
of multiplication better than another
Tom Tom rhyme.

But Mr. Hodgson takes
up all the room inside my head
and I am consumed
by imaginings.
When I think of him leaving
for his new job without me,
I look sternly at my
scholars, rap a stirring
stick across their wrists,
command them, Write:

The Tom of tarts
he stole some hearts
and took them quite away.

There's no rest for the wicked.
The Devil's own, Helen.

XIX. Fiona Thompson
Canyon City, June 1

Dearest Mama,
     Will it be
too much of a handful
having me and Bertie
waiting for Mr. Thompson
at the home place?
I believe I am strong
enough to card and spin.
You've your work
cut out for you
with Bessie, Baby Min,
Father still not
quite himself, and now me
and Grandbaby. My heart
shall sing when I see
Pendleton again.
Helen has big news, but
I'll let her write
to you herself. She's not
been good for much
these last weeks,
forgetful, always day-
dreaming. It takes her
twice as long to do
chores. Yesterday she
forgot to collect eggs
and we had a fox
visit us last night.

I am grateful for
our lodgings, but

the dampness of
cave life has settled
in my joints and I feel
my flesh turning
as toneless as clay.
You won't know me,
I've grown that thin and
I lie awake nights in fear
my own husband will
not recognize me.
My hair is limp and I've
prunes beneath my eyes.
But I bathed Baby myself today
and for the first time
didn't feel the need
to take an afternoon nap.
I cannot believe I
will be under your roof
before the jewelweed blooms.
Your eldest, F. W. T.

XX. Miss Belle Bishop
Pendleton, Oregon, June 30, 1880

Dearest Helen,
    Hopeful
that this letter finds you
in your new home amid
silver mist and fern taller
than a horse's eye. What is
mignonette and do you really
use it in place of pepper?
A diligent cold rain in June

does not sound inviting
and you may be assured
that we aren't shivering
here at Pilot Rock as
each night the sun
ignites the sage
before departing.

Many good wishes for
your impending marriage,
dear friend, from me,
Mother, George, and Peggy.
George is working
for Mr. Webb at the family
hardware; Peggy expecting
to be ill around Thanksgiving.
(Better be careful, Helen,
it could be contagious!)
Peggy still plays organ
at church and offered
to help keep shop, but
my brother told her:
"George takes care
of George" which sent her
into a protracted fit of tears.
Saw Fiona with little Berta
at church. They looked
in good health and if
there is tattle here about
her husband's defection,
I've not heard it.

Will I be the last
to wed? Will I be
last? Envy makes me
buzz from ear to ear;
sometimes I think
I have hornets caught
inside my head.
Mother says
I must take up either
hat trimming (every
woman's weakness),
school teaching (see what
backbone it gave
the little Welch girl),
or nursing like Peggy
would have done.
Idleness envies industry,
Reverend Beggs preached
last Sunday, but
shearing and washing and
carding burr-tangled
manure-caked wool until
boredom breaks your spirit
and creek cold rusts
your foot and finger joints
is not my idea of
better doing it than wishing it done.
A woman would do better
to wear a burlap sack on
her head than a hat of mine;
I cannot conquer grammar,
let alone teach it; and
I have no patience with
invalids, so feel fit

for nothing but
tending livestock.

Yesterday while moving
bleaters along Yellow Jacket Trail,
I stopped to admire
Thomas's stone animal
statues which still break
those stinging easterly winds.
I will think of you, Helen,
decorating your rooms
behind the print shop
in Olympia, Washington,
"amid the incense
of summer rain on cedars
as tattered Indian women go
door to door, bawling
mamook, mamook,
hawking clams
the size of butter dishes."
As I've said, you're clever
with words and it's not
mere fate you've married
a journalist.

Must put down
my pen now as some
ewe has lost her lamb
and rampaging through
Mama's rhubarb
making such noise
as to put the chickens
off their eggs — though
in this heat many hatch
without help.

Will you ever think of me?

Your old maid,
sheep-dip-perfumed friend,
Belle Bishop.

Book Four

INK
THOMAS AND HELEN HODGSON

*(Olympia, Washington, State Capital,
Swantown Lane, 1890–1891)*

I. (HELEN)

Diphtheria season.
Thomas goes out to sit
up all night with
the Marshville dead.
Those tattered, scab-
faced children of
godknowswhom,
sleeping in straw-filled
washtubs, assaulted by
the quaking snake-
up-your-spine feeling
of the ague since infancy.

By day, Thomas prints
funeral notices on oblong
coffin-stiff card stock,
more ink on his shirt-
sleeves than on the quarter-
inch mourning band.
Not so long ago I had
to make the soap that
scrubbed out stain . . .
Now, whenever I complain,
I stop,
shake a finger in front
of my face — what is soil
with store-bought soap
and Ol' Sal to help
on washday morning Monday?

II. (Thomas)

Editor-in-Chief, Mr. Gale, assured me
there existed many pens more
dexterous than mine, but
I was dependable and had
a healthy wife. Didn't
drink or play cards
and pledged never
to set foot through
the green braised door
of Mr. Pray's Saloon.
My first assignment: listing
passengers on the incoming stage,
a rattlebox mudwagon
up daily along the corduroy road,
through Indian Town
across Marshville Bridge
wheel rims clacking past
Public Square and Olympia's
first brick buildings —
a bank, a jail — stopping at
the pier next to
The Daily Standard's
wooden storefront
perched above the lap-lap of
incoming tide.

Inside,
ink everywhere, the floor,
the walls, on the soles of my shoes,
and splattered across two
cases of type, countless
printer's sticks, even tarring
the hand-powered press.

There's something about
ink-filled air, intoxicating
—anyone who's ever smelled it
feels the same. Paid
by the thousand words,
I average ten dollars a week,
being slow at typesetting.

III. (HELEN)

Hard to believe I'm
married years with
four tots clinging
to my apron corners.
Our wee house covered
with honeysuckle
which, in summer,
crawls through walls
into our sitting room
down the central
hanging lamp as if
reaching for one
of the shaded table lanterns
fueled by seal oil —
wicks cut and chimneys
polished weekly.
Lizarding vines aside,
I write Belle that
I'm thankful for our home and
garden on Swantown Lane
where cows roam freely
yard to yard and do
not to have to be
stalled to prevent

their returning to bands
of wild long-horned bulls
which terrified me
as a child. Here tall trees
for a tyke to climb when
menaced by rabid-eyed cattle.
Belle — married a widower
who fell in love with
her tumbleweed hair —
now helps tend a thousand
acres of yearling calves.

IV. (THOMAS)

The Commerce Page
my next assignment,
beginning with Logging Fever
in timber thick as ticks
on a bobcat's tail. A well-
trained yoke of oxen
fetches a thousand dollars
only to be spoiled by
poor teamsters and
badly greased skid roads.
First-rate bull drivers draw
four hundred a month plus
board at our finest hotel. Paid
in twenty-dollar plugs
and gambled away
at the Pray Saloon on Sundays
where — with Mr. Gale's permission —
I ventured and tried
to pen autobiographical
sketches, but amid

whiskey-tobacco slur
could not ascertain if
Till and Buck
were Mr. Shelton's
offspring or ox team.

Timber between here and
Tacoma so dense
children not allowed
in thicket alone without
horse and dog on account
the pastures of heaven cannot
be seen but in few places
along the road, a.k.a. cow trail.
The pealing of axes
at shingle mills has gone
some distance in correcting
the problem as have slag
merchants whose clippers
fill the harbor, boatholds
loaded with masts bound
for Shanghai.

V. (HELEN)

Years we lived in a lean-to
beside *The Standard*'s storefront,
our window looking out on
Wharf Row with its full quota
of liquor emporiums.
One day, my back turned
to children and bread baking
as I learned to set type.
Little Seth drew his sling-

shot and the next thing
I knew a man
with eyes as yellow
as a crow's and pupils
large as fry pans
stuck his head between
broken shards demanding
buttered bread.
When I refused, he lunged
for the door, which
I'd bolted just in time,
though his weight nearly
broke the hinges.
Tom and two printers came
immediately, but this happened
again and once a man
of the worst sort tried to steal
not my bread, but
my little Tempe.

Which is why Mr. Gale's
daughter worked the print
shop until the day before
her nuptials never to return,
and preaches that wife and
mother are job enough, but
Miss Gale received
a house with gas lights
for her betrothal and wants
for nothing but
her hats re-trimmed
by Easter.

VI. (THOMAS)

Next,
for the Commerce Page,
up Scatter Creek
to tanneries using
fir bark to cure
leather which lacks the firmness
of cowhide tanned with oak;
while seal oil rendered
on the beach below
makes harness softener —
the smell abided by but few.

What's not bog and tide-
land can be broken and
from a hat full of potatoes
an Englishman now has
eighty acres in spuds. From
a few bushels of wheat
(saved by settlers who
ate rootbread) have sprung
twice as many hectares
of weaving green so
soft a color it begs you
to rake your fingers through
like a comb.

VII. (THOMAS)

Hours of bending
over type trays, I set
paragraph after paragraph,
and early on began to care
for the little clam shell

press like a child,
foot treadle slamming
passionate kisses.
The type at first too
ardently black, then
backed off to just a peck
of gray on pure white
newsprint sheets. At night
I whittle exotic hardwood
into square and oblong pieces
of furniture to surround lead letters.
Running fingertips across
embossed alphabets, my favorite
pastime. My favorite letter?
That would be the "W"
with its ups and downs
and wings. Setting type
late into the night,
I always run out of *s*'s first,
leaving me truly
out of sorts.

VIII.   (HELEN)

Too expensive,
this cottage, but I
could not rest until
we moved, afraid
of strangers, afraid
the children would fall
off the railing into
the Sound, though I
miss the sight of snow on
oyster beds at low tide.

As the moon rose above
them . . . If I live
to be ninety I'll never
see anything like it,
especially when
Old Charlie Hildebrand played
bagpipe lullabies to soothe
his freezing bivalves.

IX. (THOMAS)

Fish commerce best left
to redmen who speak
the language of salmon
while squaws hawk razor-
back clams door to door.
Bagpipe Hildebrand,
a long-bodied, long-bearded
hungry-looking man, preempted
a hundred acres of tideland and
plays his moaning instrument
to oysters morning and late,
claiming it fattens them for
summer canning, strange
preference for a deaf man
who plays not by ear, but
by undulations.

X. (HELEN)

A new house meant I must
take in piecework from
our temperance newsletter
The Echo and, because

I'm one of the few
who knows shorthand,
transcribe election speeches
using the juice of Oregon grape
as ink. Tedious work, but
buys the June perfume
of trillium, sweet pansy faces, and
dogtooth violets
on the shade side of our cottage
where my babies
Eli and Sarah
sleep in dry goods
boxes safe from flies.

XI. (THOMAS)

I arrive at *The Standard*
before first light. Better
hours than staying up nights
with sick livestock. But
instead of selling
sacks of wool or bleaters,
we are purveyors
of mental musings
bringing on a different
exhaustion than farm life.
My hands, less callused,
and no longer oakum-
stained, now tattooed with ink.

Though a sheep may perish,
there's nothing deader than
day-old newsprint and
nothing to be done with it

but for use as wallpaper,
whereas even a ewe carcass
has value. Father says
you can't eat newsprint and
Mother's eyes agree:
Can't eat it, can't wear it, but
like wool, good for insulation,
good for heat like dried sheep
pellets and an even better way
to catch your chimney afire.

XII. (HELEN)

Our bachelor neighbor,
Mr. Knutson, and I share
Ol' Sal, a char squaw
thinly clad in garments
woven from dried cattails.
Paid in old clothes, loose
change, a cup of warm
"coppy," which makes her
rheumy eyes glisten more
than bread, and a scrap
of "cow grease." Like most
of her race, she will not
be corralled on a reservation,
but runs away
living as best she can.
Her husband, Two Colts,
looks more like a mule
with long ears and feet
the size of suitcases.
They sleep in a wigwam
near the tidelands.

Their daughter had
perfect teeth the inside bright
of oyster shells. Snow Fawn
fell victim to a lecherous cavalryman,
which is, in my opinion, what
turned the copperskins against us
more than land dispute.

When there's no wash, Ol' Sal
peddles hulled clams — two bits
a ten-pound lard pail full.

XIII. (THOMAS)

I swore to be
an editor since that day
we came into the Blues
when Mama led our horses
over a ridge and I —
I thought — aimed,
and . . . a ruined look froze
on her face and never left.
If she couldn't hear me
(was anyone really sure she'd
lost her hearing?), she could
at least read what I said.
Someday, as she wall-stared
hour by hour, it would be
my newspaper her empty
eyes fixed on, my name, my
words. What part of her soul
crawled away that autumn
afternoon? Did the bullet skidding
past her ear steal her hearing?

Or had the fright of
her son aiming a rod
at her face robbed her of keenness?
To this day, Father blames
the horses. *Confounded
worthless bays*—a judgment
on him for forsaking his oxen
when we left Minnesota.

XIV. (HELEN)

Late fall when Two Colts
ran nets, he caught a baby
seal instead of a salmon,
bringing it back to show us.
December, our Christmas
tree covered with red bags of
horehound candy and popcorn
strung on long threads
with a darning needle.
When Seth and Tempe begged
to keep it, Mr. Knutson filled
his largest tub —
being cemetery custodian,
Mr. K. was well endowed
with digging tubs — making
a seal pen. You could not help
cuddle Awk-awk, he snugged
to you soft as a bag of wool.
Now he flops behind us
following house to house,
barking for fish.

XV. (Thomas)

Concerning domestic
industries:
Mrs. Fiona Thompson,
finding herself alone,
supports her child
quite well by means of
treadle sewing machine.
Berta's time better spent
apprenticed to her
mother than in school,
easier for her to stitch
ABCs than memorize.

All in all, my Commerce Report
concludes, *paradise for the poor man*.
Mr. Gale, publisher and primary
booster of Sound Country, smiles,
eyes pinprick-polished salal berries.
I wait for him to praise me
as his splendid penman.

"It sells," he says.

XVI. (Helen)

Norwegian born,
our neighbor prays to
return home before
death shuts his eyes. There
mountains so godlike and
platinum when sunstruck
they clog the firmament.

He pines — though here
is surrounded by peaks
as ragged and protruding
as his teeth. "This chronic
rain," he mutters, "what
white man can thrive
in eternal deluge?"
For reasons unknown to me,
last winter, Mr. Knutson buried
his naturalization papers
in the cemetery.

My neighbor describes
the weather here like
the inside of *The Echo*'s dingy office:
our little hand press's roller
of molasses and glue
cooked on a rusted
heating stove. But ever since
my acquaintance with
Whispering Thompson,
I'd work for free if they
couldn't pay me. Ol' Sal
minds my children,
who follow Awk-awk
around the yard.
The sheriff's wife helps
edit. Her husband shackles
a convict Indian, bids him:
mind the young ones.

XVII. (Thomas)

Mr. Gale's new idea for
increased paper sales:
a series of biographical
sketches on Oyster Bay's
founders. Our editor,
however, embarrassed by
the wealth of detail
concerning these squawmen
wed to several copperskins
at once. My instructions: to slide
over the marriage question and
the papoose population to
Bagpipe Charlie Hildebrand,
a bachelor who *came across*
the plains by wagon from Ohio
in a year he can't remember.

XVIII. (Helen)

Echo recipe of the week:
Preventive Mouth Wash
(use on children showing
the first signs):
table salt, two drachmas; one
drachma each (then pulverize):
black pepper, golden seal,
nitrate of potash, alum.
Put into tin cup half full
of boiling water. Stir well.
Fill with vinegar. Swab
back of throat every
half hour. Allow

patient to swallow
a little each time. Apply
mixture of one ounce each
turpentine, sweet oil,
and ammonia to breastbone
every four hours.
Always keep patient
swathed in flannel.

XIX. (THOMAS)

Mr. Gale's next idea:
Almost Thirty Years After
the Assassination of Lincoln,
Local Residents Look Back . . .
But the ghoulish number
of death notices studding
the back page is now
headline news.

XX. (HELEN)

Our cottage built of boards
double-boxed, and battened.
Cracks caulked on the inside,
narrow strips of muslin
pasted over. My walls papered
with *The Standard* and *Echo*.
Our cookstove keeps us
warm with endless wood,
though fuel soggy,
dampness settling
into my bones as it does
the kindling. Coastal climate

nothing like the winters
of my childhood when
Mother walked the floor
with us to keep warm;
outside my birthplace,
snow higher than
the fence posts. First
a thaw, then rain,
another deep freeze, and
a shroud of ice cutting legs
of herder and sheep alike.

All behind me now and
Amen to that.

XXI. (THOMAS)

This month's pay affords
a clothes closet added to
our house at Center Section 9,
N. Township 3 West.
Cost: Fifteen dollars' worth
of good muslin which Helen
has on order. I thank
Providence we are able to
provide our children
the luxury of floors.
Seems like yesterday
I lived in a dugout, gravel
spread over dirt, and recall
women asking Mother if
she'd done her daily raking.
We got boards the same year
I got my first pair of laced-up

boots and stepped high
having to learn
how to walk in them

XXII. (HELEN)

Here we live on gifts
of the sea and never go
to bed hungry. My children
play with copperskins
and so do not fear them
as I did — no need to teach
my little ones how to
use an ox whip
to make an Indian bleed.
Oh, but some days I side
with Mr. Knutson:
My sugar turns to stone,
flour so damp
it makes bread
that feels like gum.
And the sky as dark
as someone holding
a Dutch oven over our heads.

XXIII. (THOMAS)

The trouble with board
floors is slivers in the feet
of tots, though Helen
keeps toes splinter free, ears
clean, keeps our little ones
walking sound and thriving:
Tempe, like her mother,

face round as a watch,
thick straight hair
the auburn of peat.
Seth favors my father,
locks like October elms,
eyes the color of the worried
sea of my first memory.
Eli and Sarah,
too soon to tell
what vine their faces
grafted onto.

XXIV. (HELEN)

Today's *Echo* recipe:
Coffee Substitute:
one gallon bran, two table-
spoons molasses. Parch
in hot oven until charred.
A tasty drink for those
who can't afford the price
of beans and if your larder
money goes for liquor
instead of taxes . . .
A sheriff's knock will be
followed by the auctioneer's
gavel, your land seized and
sold for back assessment
as Fiona's stage stop was lost
after Mr. Thompson vanished
for the last time.

XXV. (THOMAS)

Our house: parlor, kitchen,
two bedrooms, lean-to laundry
shed, and double necessary
house out back.
Down the lane to Marshville,
tiny shanties which prompted
Seth to ask, why so many
privies in this part of town?

XXVI. (HELEN)

Soaked my children's clothes
in carbolic then oven-baked
them and would like to do
the same to Thomas's suit when
he returns from a night
of sitting up. I recall
the diphtheria of my childhood:
the Bannock War
when Belle's father died,
Auntie and two-day-old
Baby Gertrude
escorted to stockade safety
only to have the wee one
smothered by diphtheria's
putrid throat. No one
seemed to know that
illness should be quarantined.
The sick must be visited,
in my mother's day —
the Eleventh Commandment.
Once, we went by wagon
thirty miles to call

on folks whose children
had taken brain fever —
first a stiff neck, then
blindness and, in their final
hours, asylum behavior.
All dead within a week.

What star watched over me?

XXVII. (THOMAS)

Sometimes I wonder what
my little ones fear. Not
losing a father to lead mines
as I did. Not running out
of matches, and so kept
nightwatch on the fireplace.
(Coals covered until
the morning smell of salt-
rising bread with its
nutty flavor of a hearth
made from sticks and mud —
the smell of my boyhood.)

Not snakes
or waiting for diamondbacks
to finish drinking from
the water dipper.
Cornhusk-colored belly,
crimson pronged tongue
thrusting out and
back. The lesson
of the drinking snake:
Did he swallow? Did he ask? Why

wasn't it his chore to haul from
the creek? The lesson
of the snake was not to
move until he returned
to the rat hole, because
after *that day* I never
picked up a gun again,
not even to defend ewe
and lamb.

Luckily, copperskins never
threatened my grazing camp,
only watched as I piled stones
into rearing antelope and
leaping hares. The edges
of Mama's mouth
rose when she saw them.
Father said they
recalled the tapestry
of a medieval hunt
which hung in the abbey
where he and Mother married.

XXVIII. (HELEN)

Up at six, soaked
children's shoes
in sheep dip and kerosene.
Egg sandwiches and lemonade
for lunch. Tempe and
Baby Eli ate only
half. Seth, I believe,
gobbled all of little Sarah's.
Foreheads cool, throats

pink as plum blossoms.
Couldn't count the funerals
Thomas had to
attend today. The perpetual
peal and slow shuffling beat
of lead clapper against
the church's iron bell.
The horse's slow four-
beat tempo pulling:
black hearse, black hearse,
white hearse to the cemetery.
It's those four white plumes
affixed to the corners
of a white coach that
wrench my heart.
Yesterday, Mr. Knutson
dug five little graves.
All Milrose children
gone, each buried
in a gaping wound-
of-a-hole leaving
a longing in their parents'
souls which nothing
but the Resurrection
can reconcile.

XXIX. (THOMAS)

In six months, final payment
on my twenty-six-volume
encyclopaedia, shipped in
a barrel by rail and dray cart
from Baltimore. I dream
of captaining my own paper,

in Seattle perhaps — though
Helen fears the influences of
rough city elements and saloons.

Mr. Gale suggests
a feature on old-timers'
impressions of *The Turn*.
Will the new century be filled
with kinescopes, talking machines,
and horseless wagons?
Straw-into-gold inventions,
Mr. Knutson calls them.

XXX. (HELEN)

The sound of spade
cutting sod kept me up
all night. Today, tried
to imagine the funeral
march for our late mayor
was the 4th of July, which
I believe the Indians
thought the case: sunrise
salute, procession up
Main, five fire wagons
followed by Uncle Sam
and the Goddess of Liberty
with 47 little girls Tempe's age
dressed in white and ribboned
with the name of state
or territory. Marching to
Town Square and a reading
of the Declaration
of Independence, then
a singing bee.

But it's barely Easter,
not early summer, and I swear
I can smell diphtheria
in the salt air. Somewhere
a mournful woman (Mrs. Milrose?)
intones "Lead Kindly Light . . ."

So tired this afternoon,
even singing fatigues me.

XXXI. (HELEN)

What would my world have
become if this afternoon
I hadn't stopped in at Sister's
and Niece's rooms behind
Fiona's sewing parlor
finding them both abed
with fever?

Wired Mother
and Dad to come at once.
Imagined a messenger
— George Bishop?—
dispatched from
the brick walls
of Webb's Hardware
to the surprise of Bessie
and Min weeding their
little scrap of kitchen
garden in front of the home
place on the dusty road
to Pilot Rock.

After propping Fiona up
in bed, her breathing
less labored,
frail little Berta, who
— though she became
comely — looks to be
not even Tempe's age
and nowhere near
as clever as her two-
years-younger cousin.
Both invalids' breath so fetid,
my first urge to clasp
my hand over nose and mouth
until all windows
could be opened.

Having snatched each
from Satan ten years
ago, how could I
leave them
at the threshold of
the Great Divide?
Regretfully put my babies
in the care of Ol' Sal
and Thomas until
parents arrive, though
Mr. Gale has commanded
my husband to write
uplifting reminiscences of
early settlers as if
the many obituaries
he composes daily
do not tax him enough.

Fiona adamant that
Mother be taken immediately
to visit Bagpipe Hildebrand
who as a child was
separated from his
overland train and picked up
near Fort Hall remembering
nothing. He's not
our brother Chipper, but . . .

Fiona's life ruled
by relentless search for
lost things, a misplaced
thimble or measure of thread
not easily borne.

XXXII. (THOMAS)

Pretended to let Old McMillan
write his own sketch:
trekking across the plains
arriving here in '52 with, quote,
a whole scalp and retain it yet
excepting the hair, which
I've lost most likely
from effects of the scare
redskins gave me:

We were as much afraid of
mulish Mormons as
of taking cholera while traveling
the Salt Lake Road.
Stopped at the tar pits,
painted our wagons with liquid coal.

As Mormons passed, they laid
many a sacred scented latter-day
malediction on our heads
— this after repeatedly trying
to steal our horses which,
according to the Apostle,
was God's will.

Gladly we took leave of
our friends, but at Soda Springs
encountered a dog-ribbed Indian
who repeatedly tried to throw
his louse-riddled buffalo
robe into the back of
our wagon, wanting to
ride with us to Salmon Falls,
a journey of "twenty-eight sleeps."
All day he called "tie-up,
tie-up," at every possession
— gun, ax, carving knife —
he coveted. Getting only
a shake of my head, he stared
at the hidden mysteries
of our campfire. Next day,
Mr. Tie-up disappeared.
After that we never had
an unbroken night's rest,
always careful to keep
out of bowshot, though
the Indians, being Diggers,
were likely unarmed.

Coming over the Blues
left our wagon

on a bluff and carried grub
to a creek bottom where
a small army of Bannocks
camped downstream.
Supposing our party famished
for vegetables, they brought
us mushrooms which we fried
and ate and thought
good as turnips, so
gathered more for breakfast.
Fixing to shave himself,
my brother went
into the fire full length, feet
in a fry pan, face on the kettle.
At first our mishaps
afforded merriment.
Dizzy, I ran into whatever
object I tried to shun;
the cottonwood on the path
to the creek knocked me down
three times before I succeeded
getting past. When we tried
to eat, it seemed
important to cram leaves
into our mouths. Chewing
and swallowing took up most
of the morning. My wife,
becoming alarmed, threw out
the mushrooms just as my brother
seized up with spasms.
Do something, she implored.
When I ran up bluff to our wagon
for tartar emetic
the sky turned red, filling

with wagon wheels. Blinded,
I had to feel for the vial,
then crawl back to camp.
I perspired profusely and in my ears
a ringing like ten fire wagons.
I could not remember how
to give antidote for
mushroom poisoning,
so administered all in one dose.
At midnight my brother's pulse
grew fuller, his spasms lightened.
After throwing up,
the red wagon-wheel sky
stopped spinning, but my dizziness
did not subside until well
into the next day and only after
I'd butted that cottonwood
like a bull each time
walking to the spring.
Two days later we found
most of our cattle stowed
in a greasewood dell, though
the gift of mushrooms
caused us to lose all our horses
to the Bannock Nation.

Here Mr. McMillan informed me
that he could go on, but
admired brevity, never
having been hung
for the practice himself.
Other than the constant
battle to keep his property
out of the hands of Mormons

and copperskins, nothing
more of consequence happened
that cholera summer of '52.

XXXIII. (HELEN)

Mama couldn't countenance
all the whiskey rats on
Wharf Row, so brought
Fiona and Berta here
to Swantown Lane, no
matter my fears of contagion.

Had a headache all day,
so could not take Mother
out to Oyster Bay to call
on Mr. Hildebrand.

Eli and Sarah grumpy
and only picking at
their barley cakes,
though did get Eli
to suck a crust
of sugared bread.
Mama scolded me
for spoiling him. Tempe's
face long after her
grandfather complained
she hummed as
she chewed stuffed rabbit
at supper. Today, fear
Seth might have caught
a chill trying to teach
Awk-awk to swim

in the creek
though I have warned
him not to go down
where railroad men
bathe and do I-know-
not-what. Thomas begged
ice for Fiona and Berta's fevers
at the Pray Saloon, but spends
nervous days writing
philosophical sermon-like
death notices wearing
out more than one
turkey quill a day.

This morning the doctor
spoke of opening
Berta's throat up
with a fishhook,
Fiona's wits scattered
too much to object.
I will not watch, I told
Thomas — such cruelizing.

The daily harvest
makes every step I take
as if through water.
The Proctor twins plus
a boy Seth played with
only last week and three
children of Fiona's best
client, Mrs. Simms:
All gone to live
in the village of
the dead. One mother

who'd just arrived
from Cleveland, packed
her two-year-old
butter-haired daughter
in a box of charcoal
shipping her home,
unable to consign her
to the rocks and lime
of our cemetery. Mama frets
over Fiona and Berta
as Father rocks on the porch
complaining about
the greasy sea air while
poking the sky with his cane
as if he could raise
the scrap-iron heavens
and this pall fallen over us.
Meanwhile, Mr. Knutson
digs graves and somehow
always finds some finery
in which to bury even
the poorest child,
God bless him.

XXXIV. (THOMAS)

This afternoon
a woman the size and
shape of an icebox
using an umbrella
as a crutch demanded
to have her say in
response to Mr. McMillan's
reminiscence. Her father,

the first white man
here at Nisqually Valley,
homesteaded in
a cedar stump.
Her first memory:
her mother uprooting
a tent pole and putting
a band of red bucks
to flight. According to
Miss McAllister the whites began
their long list of mistakes
to the Indian
in calling him "savage."
She knew copperskins
as well as anyone
and found them primitive, not
savage — until contact with
whites made them such.

I had an Indian nurse,
Miss McAllister continued,
barely giving me time to
refresh my quill. As a child
I could not do
without Indian food.
The squaws, generous
in their disposition, prepared
vast quantities and,
wasteful in nature, never
knew the meaning of
larder or *leftover*.
Their victuals toothsome,
and I am of the opinion
there would be less

sickness if we would
all take a lesson from those
old squaws. Before the whites,
there were no ailments
like we see today.
I was raised among them
and speak their language
and will say that the Indians
of today are not the ones
of my childhood; contact
with whites pocked their souls
as well as their faces.

Miss McAllister would
have stayed at my office
until darkness made
the streets unsafe,
if I had not promised
to call tomorrow
and transcribe her memories.

XXXV. (HELEN)

More news of
more fawns gone
to the Kingdom
of Stopped Time.
Thomas up all night
writing elaborate
verse of consolation
oddly interspersed
between columns
concerning ox auctions
and Secretary McKinley's
push for a gold standard.

Down the path
a family who moved
here to avoid the social
corruptions of Seattle
lost three sons.
The mother's sobs
not of this world
and she cried so
violently that I feared
she too might suffocate.
Only a pair of graves dug
as no one imagined all
three boys would go,
so two share a bed
in eternity as they did
in life. Mr. Knutson
found them velvet
jackets to replace their
flour sacking. Their lone
surviving sister
unable to understand
why her brothers' eyes
glazed like slaughtered
piglets, why they nap
now on the side of a hill
instead of at home,
and, worst, why her mother
is abed unable even
to raise a hand, let
alone take her to lap.
Thomas says
many a grave marker stolen
from the makings of
the new courthouse steps.

Tempe feverish
after dinner and little Eli
coughing louder than
Awk-awk's bark.
Fiona slightly improved
though this sickness
has taken a toll on her
already fragile lungs.
The doctor has painted
little Berta's throat with
carbolic acid, then, with
blue vitriol, pencil-burned
her neck to blood.

XXXVI. (THOMAS)

The Gospel According
to Miss McAllister:

Young man,
as I mentioned
previously, that first year
we lived in a large stump
which Father roofed;
a wagon bottom became
our door. Mother used
burned-out roots as cupboards
and hired as a nurse, a squaw.
Soon — to the mortification
of our elders — we mixed
languages and customs.
Nurse combed my teak-colored
curls tirelessly and Mother
feared I'd be stolen as my

nurse's father tried to buy me.
He had never seen a door
and could not fathom
its advantage. Why
would a white man walk
to another's home, stop, hit
the entrance, and have the owner
pull it aside? Nurse's father
felt insulted to be met
with a walled-up house
every time he visited his daughter.
And sometimes,
seeing no way to open
our door, he smashed it.
Why peck at wood like a jaybird?
He swore to us he would open
any shutter he came to and we
barred our door from that day on.
The next time he called, he gave it
a push, but it did not open.
Seizing his clam stick
he gave the door a
powerful blow bringing it
to ground. Mother,
alone inside, so surprised
she filled his legs with buckshot, but
when she saw what she had done,
dressed his wounds.
As she bandaged knees
and thighs, she broke into hymn.

Here Miss McAllister
commenced singing, her voice
the childlike ping

of fishermen's sinkers
against tin cups.

Tall stranger at the door
gently knocks, has knocked before,
waited long, waiting still,
you treat no other friend so ill.

Giving her throat a deep clearing,
she began again:

That was in the early years.
Then came measles,
smallpox, and white
colonels who did not take their
squawbrides with them
when they moved on.
One autumn night, a strange tribe
appeared at our door
holding blazing pine knots
above their heads.
The Indian slave who
had chewed my father's
food for him, shot
all our pigs and chickens.
The first lieutenant
who promised he'd drive
the copperskins like sheep,
never appeared. Out our window
redmen sharpened knives
on our grindstone.

Here Miss McAllister
put a wrinkled handkerchief

to her crepey eye.

I'll draw the curtain there,
she said; only a child at the time,
but even I could see
we'd finally met the hostiles,
mirrors
of our worst selves.

XXXVII. (HELEN)

Feeling light-headed,
a little feverish, odd things
make me giddy: lifting
this pen, the afternoon
shadow of the apple tree
stealing the brilliance of
buttercups, and a piece
of peculiar news: When
an assistant grave digger
moved two bodies,
they were found
naked and known not to be
buried in that condition.

XXXVIII. (HELEN)

Could get out of bed,
but could not
find the kitchen
at first, then
could not locate
a pot. Parents, and even
Thomas, stood away

from me, Mother's eyes
the flat color of pebbles
at the bottom of a sunstruck
creek. Father muttering,
"Must feel all right
if she wants to cook."

XXXIX. (HELEN)

Cannot raise my head.
Torture to listen
to my babies cough like
an ox who's taken
water-in-the-lungs.
Two Colts brought strings
of dried clams, but I've
no appetite and everyone's
throat so painfully swollen;
Mother pulling threads
of rancid mucus from
Baby Eli's mouth. Someone
— a Miss McAllister, with
hair like steel wool —
at the door to tell Thomas
about how the Indians
tortured her family while held
inside a cedar stump for days;
threw her little brown
dog on its side and drove
a stake through it.
"As if they could read
our nightmares . . ." Is that
what she said?

Fiona able to walk to
the porch, Berta
not looking so whey-faced,
but my own children:
now in the thick of it,
as Mother says I am.
Yesterday, felt as if
I was walking into a pond,
air dense as water; today I
trudge through mud
neck deep. What stops
this hungry contagion?
Must write Belle when
again I can hold a pen.
The news from Pendleton,
Belle's husband elected senator.
Cannot imagine the friend
of my youth, hair coiffed
and bejeweled, attending
lectures on the correct
use of fur trim. Beware,
Belle, of getting ermine
wet as there's always
a disagreeable odor
when it dries.

Mother and Fiona
outside my door
like twin spiders. I grab
at threads of conversation:
More nude bodies
— not even a shroud —
found in the cemetery.
Efforts to clothe them

as frantic as grave digging.
Something about the sermon.
Something about a lynching.
Something about a possibility
that Charlie Hildebrand
could have met others
lost and presumed
dead like Chip . . .
The missing can never be . . .
Something about the sermon
again. Dying well
assurance of ascent
into that place where
lambs never stray,
smiling lips sure proof
of a good passing.

IL. (THOMAS)

Helen cannot grasp
the gravity of it.
A false Easter Sunday
her mother told her
in explanation of
funeral guests in our parlor.
Mr. Gale, his daughter,
everyone but Mr. Knutson
who has been shackled
and kept under heavy
guard from angry mourners.
Why he stole robes
off the defenseless dead
is more than anyone
can comprehend. He paid

squaws who cooked
and kept his house
with old clothes, and always generous
to a Marshville ragamuffin.
The townsfolk are raising
fists to heaven. Every
clergyman pummeled with
the question: will the dead rise up
naked on the day of Resurrection?

Helen abed a week now,
her body a boned chicken.
Cannot let on that I feel worse
than a broken-wheeled cart.
Awk-awk searches for
Eli and Sarah, making
piteous barks. Today
Tempe and Seth, their
little arms thin and bloodless
as noodles, waved good-bye
as Two Colts took their pet
down to the shore, loaded
him into his canoe, and
paddled away, returning
Awk-awk to his habitat,
his seal eyes round and wet
as little Eli's in his
final hour.

Sleep escapes me, I
write as if on fire
as if these news columns
the broken planks of a life raft.
Words fly at me like

the ragged crows who
dog the cemetery where
I went today with two
bouquets of trillium.
Mr. Gale kindly forbade
me to write further memorials,
and his daughter Caroline
graciously granted me
a reminiscence of Lincoln.
As I try and try
to capture the voices of others,
my sorrows burn
through every line:

On Good Friday 1865,
twenty-six years ago today,
Miss Gale turned six.
Her favorite present, a playhouse
in a tree blufftop above
Astoria Bay where she watched
incoming clippers and
dreamed of being a cabin mate
bound for Canton.

Her stepmother said only boys
manned ships, so she dreamed
of firing the lighthouse beacon,
a wish also nixed. Hadn't
her father always said, if
you lose one opportunity
look for another? As ships
pooled in the pewter bay
waiting for high tide to cross
into the Columbia,

Caroline vowed to tell no one
what she'd be:
a bowsprit maiden, blond
wooden hair like a flag and
blue wooden skirts flowing;
nose to the sunset,
eye to the North Star.

Then a black spinnaker
rounded Tongue Point. Below
on the docks, ramp rat boys
dropped coiled lines.
Caroline's stepmother ran
to the porch, shading her eyes
with her hand. The entire town
stood fixed beneath
an utterly cloudless sky.
What could have turned
her stepmother's face
the color of gravel?

Soon long bolts of black
wool blew from the upper
story of every building.
Streamers hung from each arm.
Tar barrels burned.
Caroline's father set
banner headlines in the largest
black type ever seen.
Brows furrowed, jaws unhinged,
men wept openly. How had
her unspoken wish brought
the world to grief? Hadn't
Stepmother admonished her

not to harbor secrets — no
locked doors, nothing
hand hidden or
concealed in a drawer?
Whatever her willful, impudent
secret birthday wish had wrought,
she knew
(as I now know)
without asking,

that the lights in the firmament
had forever altered their course.

Book Five

WALKING IN THE SHOES OF MY NAME

*(Coeur d'Alene, Idaho, and
Spokane Falls, Washington, 1910)*

I. COUSIN BERTA THOMPSON PRINGLE

The Coeur d'Alenes, Idaho

DOT

Short for *daughter*—it was the best
they could do. Dad raised horses
near the Clearwater, freighting
to mines. February first,
three feet of snow and the cabin
burned down, though the lucky barn
was saved. The day I was born, Father
bedded Mother in the stallion's stall, moving
Old Bud in with a mare. Mother
once told me: what she remembered most
was the swish-swish of Bud rubbing his rump
against the wall next to her.

Father eventually took us to a stage stop
near the coast where I attended Miss Betty's
School.
Coming home: Mother on her hands and knees
scrubbing the pine plank floor. Grabbing
her side, she said, "Dot, a glass of water."
I called Father who told me to get
on the mule, fetch the neighbors a mile away.
I brought the water—most of it spilled—
I always wondered if that's why
she died. It's a sad thing, but
a mule cannot be hurried.

Stage stop life didn't suit Father's new wife.
After school, Stepmother waited
behind the door, coming at me

with a stick. Bloodied and torn, I had to
clean myself up, so I never found out
what I'd done wrong. She wasn't
all bad. A seamstress, she made me
the prettiest red dress,
tatted collar, sleeves trimmed in velveteen —
the only thing I dared to love.
Everyone at church said,
Isn't Dot the luckiest girl? One day Stepmother
grabbed my wrist and made me watch
as she scissored my little red dress like
chicken innards. All she said was: If you tell,
I'll drown you in the river.

Father decided I should live with my half-sister
who had a weak heart and a little
blind hermaphrodite daughter whom I took
care of while Sister's husband ran a trading post
where I also worked.
Sometimes I counted and wrapped
winesaps which wintered
in the warehouse cellar, sized russets,
turned acorn squash.
Her husband's narrow face and scraggly beard
reminded me of a parsnip. He was always
trying to get me to himself, feeling
where my breasts would be.
At night I was afraid to sleep.
During the day my sister would say, I'm so tired, Dot,
won't you take these eggs to the mercantile?
I wouldn't. *He* was there.
My sister threw up her hands, complaining
to her husband who told me:
If you say a single word,
it'll kill her.

Didn't eat much, stayed thin so I could
slide between the warehouse boards whenever
he cornered me grading potatoes. The fact
that he carried 200 pounds with only his parsnip
face able to slip between those planks was what
saved my bacon. For years afterward I dreamed
the noise of his feet climbing down the cellar ladder.
Seven rungs — that's how long I had to get away.

His assistant was twenty-four.
I was sixteen. He earned $3.50 a week. We never
let on except for stealing a kiss. Three dollars
for the marriage license, a dime for each
train ticket to Boise. I lost track of
the remaining thirty cents. All that mattered was
finally I had someone to love me.

My half-sister died, my brother-in-law was held
in high esteem — he took care of that little
hermaphrodite, who never spoke or grew,
until she was thirty. Because of
those beatings, I've always been shy
and often found it hard to hold
with public opinion.

DOLL, PIG, CAT, HORSE

As soon as I could walk I got
a doll Mama made from old underwear and
as soon as I could stand

high as a chair, Mama put a dishpan
on the seat for me to wash cups.
She gave me my own little dishrag,

doll-sized. From then on
my life was: Dot, set the table; Dot,
wash the dishes; set, clear, set, wash. Of course

I learned to sew when Dolly came unstitched,
but she could not be saved. I don't know why, but
about this time the piebald sow

took to me. She'd never had a mother.
Scratch her on the foreleg like this and she ran
alongside me with the dogs. I even

brought her in the house one day when
the Siwash came by selling berries, singing:
"Some whites buy, some

do not." Piggy and I ate *olallie* until our mouths
turned purple. This was the spring
my baby brother who wouldn't nurse was born.

Papa made the coffin, Mama lined it
with her wedding gown.
Making a pet of a pig wasn't a good idea,

you know what happens to them. The day
my hands were so chapped from washing dishes
Mama painted them with rendered fat and glycerin,

our new cat got caught in a coyote trap.
Papa offered to kill her, but I put Kitty
in the shelf under the stove where we

dried kindling — that troll cubbyhole
with a little flap-of-a-door.
Puss yowled as her broken leg

unthawed and Mama said she didn't know
if she would live through it, that cat and me,
what bawling. This was after Papa had his appendix

sutured — four days' travel to a surgeon. Biddy hitched
to the wagon, wagon to steamboat, steamboat to
railroad car. When he got home, Mama hid

Papa's clothes to make him stay abed.
I would pull Puss's lip to the side every hour,
teaspooning warm milk into her mouth. She

lived but was never strong, and had
too many kittens. By then I could stand
at the table and wash dishes and dry while I

did homework, minding my sick kitten.
Relief came when I jumped barefoot on a floor spike
and had to sit, soaking my heel in carbolic.

The minute the snow started
to leave we went barefoot to save
shoe leather. Barefoot, I rode Biddy to school.

That summer my baby brother was born
and died, I washed and cooked for
Papa's teamsters. So busy I didn't know

if I was afoot or on horseback, carrying
water from the spring which drained
into a trough too far from our door.

Between dishes and laundry and dinner,
my best school friend said, Dotty, didja know
your mama was gonna have

a baby? I said, No, and my friend said, Well,
what did you think when she got fat
and fatter? Mama's stomach

had always been a melon. Wasn't her arm flesh
the color of cantaloupe? My friend said, No one
tells you anything. I said, Do so. Just then,

Papa came in from barn chores
(already done a day's work and I hadn't
made his breakfast). He said

Biddy had found herself a little foal
in the night and the little foal was
a little bay colt and the little bay colt

was mine.

COMING HOME

Gaunt as a fishing pole,
he looked as if someone
had dumped the ash bin
over his head. But his
crimson-rimmed eyes
still flamed that same
sharp indigo.

The first thing out of his mouth:
How'd I get them six boys so fast?

Hadn't seen my father since
before my firstborn could talk.
Dad had another family
somewhere, so I don't know
why it was our woodshed
he wanted to bunk in.
Tired of the sweatbox treatment
of jailers with their offers
of bread, water, and a rockpile,
I supposed. Or bored with claiming
to confess Christ for a hard bench
to sleep on alongside a hundred
other Knights of the Open Road.

He had not lost his cussedness,
though claimed to have
turned over a new leaf
and written upon it. Ha!
He could still make me laugh.
Sam said it would be unchristian
not to take him in.

So much I wanted to ask.
He complained about my sloppy
calico and dirty apron first thing,
though not of the juiciness
of my ground cherry pie.
Why not dress myself in
flattering dandelion tones?
Were his trousers and shirt
any less raggedy, and wasn't
that a piece of rubber inner tube
instead of a belt? The plug
he chewed stained his whiskers yellow.

Like everyone else
on the knife-gashed canyons
of the Coeur d'Alene,
we'd invested in mountain-
side holes hoping for a strike.
Meantime, Sam drew wages
haying alpine hills.
I'd just got back from taking
him to Highfield when my
second youngest, who wasn't
quite chore broke, said he saw
Santa Claus walking door to door
asking for our family by name.
I told him, Stop lying or
I'll give you a session
with a trunk strap. The two
oldest had been down
under the new steel trestle
hunting pigeon, selling
to the butcher at Post Falls.
(I had a pair of rabbits out back
that fetched about the same for
baby bunnies, so we wouldn't starve.)
Right then the twins came
in from playing marbles between
cinder beds stretched
amongst the iron trackage.

I'd so much to ask him,
but in no time he'd charmed
even the baby. Earning a dime,
he told my boys, the easiest thing
for a child, requiring just
a little cunning and best

accomplished on the fertile
plank sidewalks in front
of an ale house. Take
along the youngest, he told
my firstborn, or the loudest bawler.

Up to my elbows
in biscuit making, I left
a flour-marked trail, kitchen
to stoop, trying to listen in.
He told them: Find yourself
a saloon with a good bit-o-crack
between sidewalk planks, then
bend over, fish amongst the boards,
using a piece of wire if
you can get it. And I thought,
if he stays, how will I feed?
The junk man pays a little for scrap —
barbed wire, rusty horseshoes.
I always scoured the roadsides
driving Sam to haying.
Bottles brought one long bit a dozen,
a single gunny bag, the same.

That's when I noticed how
milky his eyes, the red
blotches on his skin. He hadn't but
a few teeth. He told my boys —
five little fawn heads, plus
the baby in an apple crate —
fish the cracks, then get
the little one to bawl.
When a patron asks what
you's all about, tell 'em you lost

your only dime down there.
He told my boys to call him
Whisperin' Bob, not Grandpa
which made him feel old.

Works every time, he said:
Spokane's thirty whiskey mills equals
thirty dimes, better wages than your pa!
My boys rode their stools
around the porch after him the way
Dad and Hookey Burke
used to ride their horses.

I didn't see a flask; safe, I thought,
to leave him with my little ones
while I harnessed the mules
to pick up Sam, taking
the baby along — you never knew
what an Indian might swap for.

As I buckled breeching,
affixed the shafts,
I wondered why he'd
left me and Mother
so many times, and was it true
that I was an unrecorded child?
After Mama died, he'd taken
me to live with him, but
why had he sent me to
my sick half-sister's
when his new wife left
— that other family again —
never saying a word
to Auntie Helen or Gramma?

By the time they found me,
I'd married. What had he done
with their letters, the money they'd sent?
Or with Mama's lace tablecloths
and pewter serving tray —
grape leaves hammered
into it, so real-looking you'd
think it was an arbor at hard frost.
Mother's wedding gown,
I remembered, got used to dress
my baby brother's coffin.

I scoured the aspen road to Highfield,
finding only two dusty bottles
and a greasy flour sack for the junk man.
Sam said if Dad stayed, he could
teach the boys to whittle. And I
thought, yes, I could make soap
cakes and the boys could carve
them into shapes — horses, sheep,
selling to summer people
who frequented Spirit Lake. And
because soap was white, my eyes
lit on the white aspen trunks, then
the white light gleaming on an emerald
expanse of lake. My world
shimmered pure and I thought, yes,
I *can* feed, he *will* stay, and
when snow comes, the drifts
will keep this same cheery light.
I hadn't felt so happy since
I met my husband.

When we turned into the yard,
my children scattered across
the road like frightened fowl.
I asked, Where's your grandpa?
My oldest said, In the kitchen
puttin' up an awful fuss.
Damn-it drunk, I thought,
my hackles raised.
There he lay, face up,
glaring at the black cookstove
I loved so much because
of what I could make it do
when I had enough flour and sugar.
His waxy face tarnished the milky
light that filled my heart.

Sam hoisted him onto the table.
I laid him out. Later we discovered
he hadn't a penny and a charity
in Post Falls had to help bury him.
Sam promised me: When
miner's pick brought down the white
ash of our long-sought strike,
white marble would grace
my father's last address.

II. TEMPERANCE HODGSON WICKE

Spokane Falls, Washington

SPILLAGE

I'm stupid about pig killing, but
Howard's cousins knew everything.

Mostly I cut lard and cleaned intestines.
It took days of scrape
and wash, turn, scrape again, rendering
perfect sausage casings.
All in all I'd rather be
washing lantern chimneys. And
always Mother Wicke would call: Watch
the rice pudding doesn't burn.
One of the cousins, Lil this time,
mocked her, then ran to the stove.

Husband Howard gone all day
to the bank, golfing on weekends.
I used to caddy for Father, but wives
aren't allowed. In high school,
I'd wanted to nurse,
but Father feared the naked
bodies of men would spoil me
for marriage. At the university,
I took a normal degree
and taught near a dying
silver mine. Wild cattle ran
out of bunchgrass hills through
sea-of-mud streets to the river.
Nighthawk City, not one painted building.
Some scholars came to school hungry
and without lunch pails. One girl
never wore shoes or coat
and coughed so loudly I couldn't
shout over her. Another couldn't
see the slate no matter how
large the chalk letters.
I took my scholars down to the creek
and cooked fudge every day for a week.

Accused of stealing sugar,
I was fired,
sent home to Olympia, where I set
newspaper type. After too many
proofreading errors,
Mother said I was so keen
with numbers I ought to keep books.
Making bank deposits,
I met my husband.

Howard brought me to these palomino
windswept hills where people
are so crazy for wheat
they plant nothing else,
though Father Wicke
has forty acres in sugar beets,
but no reliable labor to tend it.
Mother Wicke's chickens
and lard the only local dairy
as Uncle Fritz's Herefords
the source of typhoid, so slaughtered
and gone. Their pasture sold
to Tudor homes with carriage houses
big as a fifty-cow barn.

Carrying kerosene lanterns to bed
every night, my job to wash
chimneys and clean wicks.
What a joy when power
poles and the fireless cooker
arrived. I thought I'd never
have to bake beans again. Nothing
could make the Kelvinator
burn that slow though Mother Wicke's

rice pudding recipe thrived,
the skin over top thicker than ever.

Out of breeze, out of bathwater,
a windmill powered the well, but
the dried grass manes of these
Palouse hills were never still.
When the Chinooks swept over us and
into Spokane, the rust-red city clanked
against lead-blue hills.

Sausage making the first day,
scrapple the last. Lard
melting in the iron kettle
between barn and icehouse.
Carefully stirring until everything
melted smooth as taffy, I poured
lard into little one-pound tins ready
for Mother Wicke's pie making.
I'd never known people
to eat so many sweets.

At the tail end of pig slaughter,
we began watermelon pickle,
and that's when I opened the hundred-
pound sack of sugar.
In Nighthawk, a bag of sweetener
had been part of my wages,
and I assumed I could put it
to any use that I wished.

After butchering watermelon
the pig-gut-like innards brought flies
thicker than mud splatter.

Pots took up every burner.
I sprayed Flit on the floor,
the stove, canning jars, the sugar.
The miracle of insecticide
prickled my nose.
That afternoon on the verandah,
heat snakes crawled beyond the mulberry
shade across the road to the river.
Our lemonade tasted queer
as did the pie and chilled tea.

Come evening above Edison Gold
molded records on the phonograph,
men spat, sucking cigars, none taking more
than a sliver of cake. They spoke
over Beethoven's flutes
of Spokane streets in winter — worse
than crossing Lake Coeur d'Alene.
As Father Wicke proposed
chaining vagrants to break rock
for paving roads,
I knew what had to be done.

Somehow I got that sugar
sack up to the third floor
where I laid newspaper —
an issue Mother had sent
featuring Father's editorial:
Sunday closures and banned
liquor emporiums. On top
of my parents' fierce mental labor,
I spread granulated sugar.
The fragrance of Flit at first
overpowering, then slowly waned.

Later that week, on rice pudding night,
the last day of pig killing,
Mother Wicke's recipe never
tasted better. I served as instructed:
a little skin showing on top
of each serving, no portion too runny,
a spoonful of hard with every
spoonful of juice, all arranged neatly
in the plate's center with
not one drop of spillage.

WHEN I TOLD FATHER I WANTED TO STUDY NURSING

He said it would be like
the sod house he learned to build,
asked: Temperance, what good?
Are you a Sister of Charity,
a missionary, is there a war
I don't know about?
I didn't raise you
to work in the streets.

I argued (my willfulness again):
Yes, like the soddie he'd helped
build as a child, hadn't it saved
his life? Hadn't he once told me
he took to it like a calling?

What good such knowledge?
My Eiffel Tower father,
weather vane arms outstretched,
spinning in fury — not at me, I see now,
a dozen years later.

Careful, he always reminded,
of sandy soil, it makes worthless bricks.
The best sod cut
from buffalo wallow, broken
by grasshopper plow,
a cutter fin attached to the share.
Have I told you, Temperance,
that when we first came
to this country, we hadn't
horse or implement and broke
ground by spade? Did I tell you that?

You've never seen the oak and elm
Isle of Man. When my family left,
we followed the example of squirrels
who, without trees, burrowed
like groundhogs.

Father's backward glance
blazes at me still:

Tempe, you can't know
what it was like. Only two willows
at the spring in the draw
where we camped. One
became our ridgepole. For rafters,
not even a cornstalk and so
used sunflower stems.

The sod must be moist if not
thoroughly soaked.
Cut to a depth of two inches.
Remember, wet turf settles;
the best grass, leek-colored
and coils like carpet.

Did I tell you, Tempe,
that I carried sod rolls
by handbarrow, a child
not old enough to go to school?
Did I tell you that it nearly
killed me, but later
saved my life: My arms
compensated for rickety legs.

Each brick placed grass side down,
two sods' width to a wall.
Don't forget, tie your corners,
break your joints, bind
the sod bricks with mud and mortar.
The weakest spot in a wall, the corner.

For roof sheathing we made do
with what brush we could find —
hay for the ewes too precious —
then shingled up with sod. If only
we could have used the wagon cover
for a ceiling. When it rained
mud wouldn't have fallen across
our supper and Grandmum's red quilt.
If only the eaves could have been wider
to protect our walls from rain.
Temperance, remember: if grass grows
on your roof, you're blessed;
roots mat, shedding water.

We hadn't a stove —
just as well, we couldn't afford stovepipe.
Later when we left, walking West,
I saw milk cans used as chimneys.

Our fireplace sod, the floor dirt.
My job to dig clay from the buffalo wallow,
paint the floor, letting it cake
into a hard covering
that would not wear away.

When we had newspaper,
we jollied the inside walls while
mice dug through the roof.
Centipedes . . .
Once we woke up to a snake
curled on the windowsill.
My father made our door hinge
from a broken piece of harness.
I don't believe it had a latch.

Warm in winter even if
all we burnt was braided straw.
I never saw a dipper frozen
into a water pail until
I came West, except once — when
a draft blew through a rat hole.
We'd no colds or sickness. Then

I came as far as one could walk
into the setting sun. We tried
building a soddie at Pilot Rock,
but desert grass too thin and sandy
soil can't hold the shape of a brick.
What's such wisdom worth when
good ground can no longer be found?

Child, you've a clever mind.
I didn't raise you to nurse,

most illness spawned
by wickedness and vice.

What can I say to get you to mind
the lessons of my youth?
Leek roots in buffalo wallows
made a house that, with care,
would never fall, but
in a century without virgin sod,
we must look elsewhere
for the knowledge that keeps.

WALKING IN THE SHOES OF MY NAME

I remember the first time
away from home and school and relatives:
straight out of the normal
on teaching assignment. Nighthawk,
I boarded in a scholar's home, my quarters
a lean-to off the kitchen shared
with potatoes and sugar sacks.
I'll never forget lying on my cot,
staring through the hole where a stovepipe
ought to be. Studying Orion, I thought
of my recent visit to Auntie Belle.

Not my graduation present, but
my brother's. Traveling didn't
suit Seth and since I hadn't
a single proposal . . .
Even as a child, trains
terrified him and Seth would not leave
the waterways of Puget Sound.
I hadn't seen Auntie since

grammar school when
her pewter-haired husband
got elected a U.S. senator.
What did I know of her? Just whispers:
Belle, Godblessher,
a genius with cattle, but
that crimson tumbleweed hair and
a complexion the same color.
Anyone with an orphan calf had given it
to Belle who'd take a nurse cow,
spread cow wee on the newborn's back,
bonding suckling and surrogate.
Famous on the Umatilla, though
the cousins made eye rolls at her
divided skirts, plug hat,
snakeskin, knee-high
buccaneer boots. For years I thought
Godblessher part of Auntie Belle's name.

Five days to cross the continent.
Somewhere near the end
of the train, lampblack cars where
third-class passengers heated
sandwiches on an unreliable stove.
Mine, the red parlor Pullman, living
palms at each end. Sleeping berths
and hot towels bore me
to flat muggy Washington, D.C., where
the sun rose over
a putty-colored river.
Every building a granite monument.
My hometown a state capital, but this!
Nothing prepared me.

I wrote Seth, who studied the dialect
of buildings: Auntie Belle's home
on Embassy Row has not one
spider; if you inspected this house
you'd not break into sweats.
Four imported marble fireplaces,
carved California redwood
in the butler's pantry, a solarium filled
with tangerine trees. Frescoes studded
a spiral staircase up to sixteen rooms
and servants' quarters. Imagine, Seth,
your own elevator; Orion painted
on the ceiling above a birdcage door.

I wrote Mama: Ladies in kaleidoscope
costumes, bare-necked, bosomy,
many like Belle without children,
all holding seminary certificates.
In their kitchens, stoves
as big as bedrooms. Everyone thought
my degree from territorial college
a novelty; intrigued by stories
of Awk-awk my pet seal and
Ol' Sal our Indian char girl.

Listening to wit peppered
with Byron and Gorky,
I remained too timid to speak —
A co-ed from the far west
by name Temperance, surely
bound for the front lines
of sobriety laws and
the equal suffrage amendment.
How wonderful (I can still see

their mouths opening wide
on the *won* of won-derful,
the chorus's few broken teeth
perfectly mended in gold). Won-derful
to be born into a time when women
would have equal say and men
didn't drink. Won-derful to walk
in the shoes of my name.

Auntie Belle, noticeable as a fire wagon,
never outdone in tiger-striped
shirtwaists drowned in tidal waves
of ostrich plumes. Was I off to Brussels
or Constantinople? Not one
downturned mouth at the sight
of my naked ring finger.

To Father: a letter describing
bad-smelling men wound in bed-
rolls like sausages sleeping
in gray cobbled streets wide
as the Nisqually; men
at the back door begging bread,
please, Misses, with a scrap of lard.
All fed, but not before
they chopped wood, though some
with tremens so bad
you'd be committing murder
putting an ax in their hands.
And what streets, Father, not one
mud splash. Never scraping
filth from my hem, no need
for an extra handkerchief
to wipe splattered shoes.

Or for hat netting to protect
my cheeks from dust.

Strange never to see teepee camps
as if redmen had died out or fled.
Instead, slave children, some
in jackets so shredded they looked
Army-of-the-Potomac issued. On our way
to an exhibition of men in wood-
and-canvas-winged gliding machines,
our carriage jogged through pocked
unpaved streets in the middle of town,
unpainted stoops dotted with black
arachnid people, the bare branches
of the elms their laundry dried in
thin as their spider arms.

To Gramma and the cousins: I described
sit-down dinners for twenty-four,
in sturdy-as-a-horse brocade chairs.
The hotchpotch speech of foreigners,
their furs — men in sable down to
their boot tops, even though the air here
greasy as a kitchen at doughnut-frying time.
And always at night, opera or
a play by Oscar Wilde.
(What would the cousins say?)
Velvet-curtained theaters branded
in *fleur de lis*, crowned by gilded
acanthus contrasting the bleak brick
buildings of Belle's daytime hours spent
at the Door of Hope Mission and
Florence Crittendon Home.

From between the frills
of my writing desk, in the cabbage-
rose-wallpapered guest room,
I wrote the State Normal,
testing the power of my name, and
received immediate assignment.
Nighthawk, population 100.
Temperance. I accepted no diminutive.
The wings of my pledge
carried me back West to the sand-
bars of an underchurched town
on the Similkameen, shadowed
by bunchgrass hills no one thought
to plant with wheat, the noise
of pick and black powder
drowning what songbirds
the quicksilver hadn't killed.

Miss Puffed-up Temperance Hodgson
fresh from her District of Columbia
graduation trip
presided over curious eyes
pressed to knotholes. Chinks
in my schoolhouse walls so large
the woodstove couldn't cope
any better than I. My best arithmetic
scholars working as faro dealers by night.
Walking home from lessons, I followed a trail
of playing cards strewn along streets,
losers discarding aces and old kings
in the hope of changing their luck.

In a lean-to room filled with enough spiders
to drive my brother deep into his cups,

I slept fully clothed for warmth, staring
at Orion through the stovepipe
hole in the roof, remembering
painted stars on the elevator ceiling
of Auntie Belle's house.

The town fathers hoped my name
would bring discipline
to North Star School.
I'd not one soulmate there and
could not write of my failures to anyone.
Sad to say, Oscar Wilde's death
Good News in the Mission Field of Nighthawk.
Above my bed, my only comfort —
the stalwart hunter's diamond
belt and shield, his spear like my name
forever brighter than all others.

RELATIONS

It isn't true that I fell asleep
on my egg route the day Mama,
Cousin Dot, and Gramma arrived,
though those mules have brought
many a drunk-to-stupor hired man home.
I'd knocked myself witless
— three dozen to Sacred Heart Hospital,
and when I slipped on the moss rot
of steps, everything but that basket
landed wrong — so when I asked
our foreman to pick up my relations,
he was quick to judge my condition
as kin to his own. Half hour's jog
into Spokane across the steel

Monroe Street Bridge
past the new additions with streets
named for trees, for presidents,
for birds, for letters of the alphabet,
when the names of children and wives
ran out, to Wicke Homestead
on a windy rock-and-pine-speckled
bluff above Kettle Falls.

Woman chatter sang above the click
of dusty shoes against gravel.
Coming across the courtyard,
I heard Mama ponder which
the most soothing, kindliest flowers?
Which would wave and
beckon you, *come hither*?

Later Gramma Welch said, Imagine
an indoor back house kept clean
as a parlor, a marble shower.
All women agreed: a room for laundry
wonderful for modesty's sake.
So many copper tubs and
a hired man to turn the wringer.
I make apologies like Hail Marys for
this holy altar of a new white enamel
Kelvinator fireless cooker
in the kitchen of Howard's
parents' big brick house.
Mama said, Imagine
(Imagine, Imagine — exclamations
like church chimes), Imagine
putting up gingered pears
without the heat of Hades.

Whenever Mother, Cousin,
and Gramma visit, their expressions
(even Dot's thick tongue) ask:
Why so many rooms? A three-
story house with kitchen plumbing,
pipes painted white, peeling
when heated and needing repainting
every six months (which might
answer the question of what
I do with all my time).
And—those cursed pipes—
Howdy's mother's eyes
flying to a dandruff of paint chips
blanketing our communal floor
never oiled well enough
and so dark they show
like the first snow.
To my family I apologize
for my Marie Antoinette life,
while feeling like a refugee
from the Spanish-American War:
Our living quarters on the north
side of the second floor,
sitting room a walled-in porch,
our furniture, kitchen gear,
even clothes and sheets divvied out
by Mother Wicke, not what
I'd bargained for after I quit
teaching to marry a bank teller.

I offer cake.
The queen of France would have
pleased my mother, hair so
high, fuller than mine, my skirts

too skimpy, wandering
around the house all morning
in a kimono. Mother hints,
what joy to have a baby and go
to bed for a month — the only
rest she ever got. I should never
have let it slip that I wanted
only two children; tampering
with God's plan,
the church of Beelzebub
in Gramma's book — along with
elevators, moving stairs, and
indoor privy porcelain bowls
with holes punched into their bottoms.
I want to ask, What happened
to the church of God-helps-those-
who-help-themselves?

Tidying the first-floor parlor
before afternoon sun javelins
dust into the Turkish carpet,
these women wonder if the blooms
of jonquils and black-eyed Susans
would endure. Would they wave and
beckon, *come hither?*
I show Mother where we stow
pies under the sofa,
the coolest place,
this parlor only for summer
afternoons. Checking
rhubarb-berry pastries
for evidence of mouse pills,
I set more traps.
The three stand behind me

in the kitchen doorway, watching
as if touring Versailles —
arms hanging loose,
fingers tugging at mauve
linen skirts wrinkled into tracks
like the iron rails
that brought them here.
Dot pulls a handkerchief
from her sleeve. Their
conversation resumes:
whose turn to freshen the flowers?
Cousin suggests Shastas.
Mama says she cannot
bear their bald white centers:
yellow disks of ox-eyed daisies
such cheering comfort to a grave.

THE LITTLE REFINEMENTS OF LIFE

July 5th: in Howard's boss's Maxwell,
set out on our first auto drive to the coast.
Packed lunch for three and a spare
pair of white gloves.

During thundershowers, pulled
the top up, leather like new harness
without the smell of horse.
Heading south, we rolled through
Palouse wheat and sugar beet.

Moses Lake: hit a hole at top speed,
ducked under the windshield,
shrouds of jaundiced water covering us.
With my body, sheltered the lunch box

and spare pair of gloves.
Stopped to dry off — faces parched,
lips lined with dust.
Howard took a turn, but
did not release break or clutch
to Mr. Monc's liking,
sending the bank manager into fits.

The men talked of tires,
foreign investments in rubber.
As we negotiated the Rattlesnake Hills,
our right hind exploded.
By now my stockings had cornrows,
rocks in my shoes; thought
I'd bounce out of my seat, my insides
like Kettle Falls where four tributaries meet.

Heading for Cle Elum,
bothered by punctures. Mr. Monc decreed,
Drive on. What discomfort fixing flats.
Another tire flew off just outside Roslyn.
Barely able to pull, zigzagged on rims.
Mr. Monc spied a barbed-wire branding pen,
asked if I'd packed pinchers.
Of course I had not.
With tire iron and stone, broke
the fence, which he directed wound
around brims, anchoring through spokes.
All the way to Tacoma, spun
on barbed-wire wheels.

Never felt so gritty riding
astride or by stage, so with triumph
pulled on new gloves the fresh

white of soft lard. Mr. Monc,
judging my royal hands as
too idly clean, asked, What use
females on motorcar trips?

THE FLOOD

Sitting on Father Wicke's verandah,
cleaving to the lilac beside the steps,
I sucked the flower's smoky shade,
and tried to remember the first time
I'd known it had been Drover,
the narrow-as-a-shadow hired man.

It was the day Mother Wicke
took away all the ties I'd bought
for Howard: too dark a blue.
Howdy said I should have
sympathy for her — losing
a child made life harder to bear.

We'd had a spell of rain,
mud about six inches deep and
the color of a brickyard.
A wind came from the south
which should have warned us.
Mother Wicke's black walnut
blew down the night before
and she'd wept all day.
I'd always hated that tree; acid
resin dripped from each
coffin-shaped leaf, nuts harder
than wood knots, and the hulls
stained my hands worse than ink.

That night when Howard and I
went up to our room,
it came to me: Never another autumn
would its dead leaves litter
the drive smelling worse
than wet buffalo hides.
Black walnut-molasses pie
had been Howard's sister's favorite.

Something woke me.
The metallic glint of Howard's watch?
My husband rose at dawn, helping
Father Wicke in the orchard
before work at the bank.
Yesterday it rained nails and
they'd quit picking even though
apple perfume drowned out the stink
of skunk cabbage at Hangman's Creek.
I went to the window, stared down
at the fallen walnut, wondering
at the water's silvery halo.

"Move fast, think faster!"
Mother Wicke's splay-toed
sparrow feet tick-ticked behind me
down the stairs.

Out in the yard burls had escaped
the woodhouse and bobbed
about as if alive, the river
up to the second rail
of the barnyard fence.
I told Mother Wicke and Howdy
I'd run out back,

warning the hired men.
Corncobs, kindling, cow pies
floated everywhere
and made mean walking.
Up to my thighs in water so cold
I fully expected
to be cut by floating ice.
When I turned past the smoke-
house, the current nearly
broke me in half.
Most of the banties clung
to the roof of the gabled
chicken coop, once Howdy's
sister's playhouse. A pair
of spotted rabbits huddled
atop the woodpile.

Water covered Tully's stoop
as well as the foreman's
bare feet, his white hair burning
in the light of a fishhook moon.
Even through flood spray,
he smelled of fried sowbelly
and whiskey and seemed
not to concern himself
with my warnings.

I hadn't thought about what
I was doing, just waded
through mush toward the higher
ground of the orchard,
pulled by invisible line.

They say Mother Wicke wouldn't
let Tully cut down the rope
which finally rotted,
blown away in a dust devil.
I don't know why, but
I had to see the tree.
There'd been rumors of
a young man, Howdy's sister
never said who.
Then elopement, they'd thought,
right in the middle
of sugar beet harvest. New
Japanese labor brought in, men
closer to the ground, better able
than Anglos to bend over for long hours.
Father Wicke scoured the county.
Three days later when he went to prune
the orchard, he found her.

I tramped past workers' bare
board huts, a privy listing
into the tide; my white
nightdress clung to my body
like skin. I'd lost a slipper.
My hair dripped.
Hired men surged past me.
Only one, silent as a tow sack,
leaned against the back
of the bunkhouse, taking
shelter under an eyebrow of eaves,

Drover.
If he had another name,
not even Father Wicke knew it.

Rook-eyed, rook-headed,
he stared into the orchard
past an uprooted quince.
I followed Drover's gaze
to a Bellflower apple,
one of the first Father Wicke planted.
I don't know how, but
I knew it was him.
Tall for a Spaniard, he spoke
only to horses. A bronc buster,
he touched the reins gently, sitting
on a cayuse as if sewn
onto the saddle.
I noticed him the first day
I came here — fawn-tempered
and shy as a beaten dog.

I called: Drover, come to the house,
Mother Wicke says so. I might as well
have been speaking to a wheel spoke.
His eyes never left the apple tree
nearest the neck-yoke bend
in the creek where, in May,

forget-me-nots mirrored
the color of heaven.

ANNALEE IN SECOND SIGHT

Whenever a team of high-
stepping bays trots down
Hangman Creek Road,
Mother Wicke says, If only
Annie could see,
she came to love horses so.

I never met my husband's sister.
In tintypes, freckles pepper
a toadstool nose and buttermilk skin.
Hair perhaps the color of wheat, curls set
with egg white, wound up in rags
at night. Cousins Lil and Eppie
called her honey-natured, said
she was never one to burden
others with her cares.
In the kitchen, weights and measures
confounded her, though at supper
Annie always served seconds
of scrapple and pumpkin butter or
whatever a guest had a tooth for, saving
something special for Drover and
the hired men who tore
at their food like feral dogs.

Midday, too hot even to read
a novel, Annalee's face appears
beside my hammock.
I close my eyes against mosquitoes,
but Annalee does not fade.
Dressed as she might have been
on the day she died five years ago:
brown riding skirt, boots
laced with rawhide strings,
her hair tied up under a straw bonnet.

This scene plays out in front of me:
Drover and Annie
groom Chehalis, my husband
Howard's fastest horse,
red neck set high on his chest,

arched like a rainbow,
forelegs thin as Drover's
terra-cotta arms.
As they bathe Chehalis
for the big race,
Annalee holds the stallion's
knotted rawhide rope.
Beside them a rain barrel,
just-cleaned brushes
drying in the sun.
Drover bends down,
picks up each of Chehalis's hoofs,
digging out packed mud
with a tiny iron pick. Annie points
to objects, pronouncing their
English names: wheelbarrow, manure
fork. Drover's Spanish tongue
hammers at the words like a blacksmith
fashioning a shoe. Annalee pours
a small bucket of water over
the horse's hocks, lead line
in one hand, pail in the other;
she holds a boar bristle brush
between her thighs, making
a dent in her skirt as if
wearing trousers.
Without thought, without
the slightest hesitation,
Drover's reedy fingers
— his are the hands of a pianist,
not a wrangler — pull
the brush from between Annalee's
legs, sweeping it across
the stallion's coppery flanks.

Here, time stops.
The couple holds their breath.
The green flecks in Annie's
irises turn to glitter as they
meet the ripe figs in Drover's eyes.
Their heads jerk away, gazes
flying in different directions.
Chehalis snorts, shies at
the sudden motion of
Annie's shadow. Without
words, as if rehearsed, Drover
takes the lead from her,
quiets the stallion as the master's
sister stands out of range
of the strike of iron shoes nailed
to Chehalis's rearing hoofs.

I fan myself with a corner
of my apron, wave away the biting
flies. Open my book, close it.
Again see his sienna fingers reaching
toward the narrow folds in her habit-
cloth skirt for the boar bristle brush
as if reaching for her hand.

I close my eyes; the past exhausts me.
Drover will meet me in a year's time.
To Annalee, I am but a name in a letter.
By August, he will pretend to have
forgotten all the English
she has taught him. By apple harvest,
it is certain: she will never kiss
my cheek or welcome me as *sister*.

STONE LAMBS

Everyone remarked how well
I took it. My husband sobbed and
Mother Wicke sucked her lip
as I asked to hold
my stone lamb. From among white
sheets and walnut bedposts,
it was I who reassured them:
Better this way
little pinched eyeslits below
brown bunchgrass hair,
spiky straight when it
dried. Why, hours after,
did her ability to absorb
my warmth surprise me?
Miniature toe and finger nails
the perfect white
of a just-born calf, before hoof
trods soil. No, I couldn't
give her up,
not after my eye caught the mirror
wink of a blade falling from Dr. Biltz's
black bag — calfskin notched
like lizard. Outside my window
in the dusty livery yard, the blacksmith
punching nail holes into an iron shoe
and the raucous noise of Drover,
the part Indian, part Spaniard hired man,
name-calling another.

There were early signs, but
so filled with anticipation,
I failed to read first
the ill freak of heavy snow, then

the freeze and thaw across
pine-studded hills to the treeless
scablands beyond the Spokane.
At night the noise of frantic cattle
pawing glazed-over water holes;
my lamb lay cramping my heart
and I waited for a flutter.

My belly rose like bread
during a cold spring vacant
of the *oo-loo* of prairie chickens,
their barred wings seldom spreading
across the Palouse's undulating green
hills which before June turned
the olive color of sage, grass
bent to the ground by gray
volcanic dust. From the fields
the only sound the coughing of cattle
and the terrible rattle of snakes
hidden beneath buckthorn.
By July, hardly a choir of yellow
sunflowers anywhere.

Better this way. That my stone
lamb never breathed, instead of
robbing the heart like Eli and Sarah.
As a child, I refused to play dolls,
their china cheeks too much like
the waxy faces
of my dead brother and sister.
And I'll always remember
the way my porcelain-faced babies,
sprawling limply on the pillow
of my girlhood bed, bore

into Mother's heart. The day
after the double funeral,
I shelved them behind glass. Forever
saved, everyone said, for my own
little ones' play.

Now my in-laws tiptoe near,
grasp my bloodless hand, powdering
me with kind whispers of
Now it's time to give her up.
Outside my window, Drover
and the other hired men —
slaughtering snakes or
knifing each other?
I cannot hand her over
to the butcher, carving blade hidden
in his black witch doctor's sack — as if
draw-and-quartering another living thing
will give up the mystery of stillbirth.

If I had the energy to speak,
I would tell them: Answers
do not make death anything less.
The day my brother and sister
perished from putrid throat,
Mother penned in her diary:
Overcast, drizzling rain.
Eli went first just before church
bells rang out the noon,
Sarah followed at about three.
After that, Mother only wrote
about the weather in her diary.

Exhaustion breeds its own
brand of mental clarity.
They will do what they will
with my lamb, but I'm steadfast,
and will not hand her over.
So weak I cannot move my tongue,
my eyes say: You'll have to
pry her from me.
I turn away, gazing out the window
across withered fields
and a cloudless sky, today
for the first time clear
of prairie fires.
The cracked gray soil,
which would be black
for want of rain, speaks to me:
that's how I feel, sucked dry like that.
I grip my hand around my lamb
and strain my ear for the faint
music of Kettle Falls, reaching
for the soothing message of water.
As they pull her away,
my gaze fixes on the dust
of the stable yard
near the barn wallpapered
with the skins of diamondbacks.
Ranch hands drape fresh-
killed snakes limp as clothesline
over the fence rails, then stop,
gather around Drover
who's gashed his arm. He lifts
a snake head to the scarlet wound,
dripping clear venom
into slashed flesh. The others —

so covered with dust they're
all one color — hang back, pushing
boot toes into gravel. No one else
tries the poison cure.
Dr. Biltz follows my eye,
disapproval wrinkling his lined forehead
as heavy brows run into each other
like the furrowed gray hills where
this year wheat refused to grow.

No Nez Perce ever died of venom,
other than from a whiskey keg.
Tomorrow Drover's knife wound
will be neither red nor swollen.
Life. Death. Stone lambs.

Some things are not to be
explained.

Book Six

COME SIT BY MY SIDE IF YOU LOVE ME

(Washington State, 1933)

I. TEMPE

Spokane, Washington

Last night,
the art of dressing in white
on my mind and
my twin bride-to-be daughters.
Their short figures made awkward
by full flaring skirts?
Head aching from indecision,
I dreamed Aunt Fiona
alive, hand-sewing
the girls' wedding gowns,
her flitting fingers white
cabbage butterflies,
each tiny silk stitch
equally spaced.

I'd forgotten
her chiming laugh.
In my dream, as in memory,
her sparrow face, carefree —
she of so many cares.
What ancestor bequeathed her
an airy nature? Grandma Welch's
expression dour as a falcon.
Mother with a liquid ox-like
steadfast eye. In my dream
Aunt Fiona lost a needle
while basting pleats and
could not rest until she found it.

I'd forgotten that about her, seeker
of misplaced trinkets. Mother said

her sister searched all her life
for their lost brother
and now must be united
with him in heaven. If only
she were here to sew
heirloom taffeta *chine*.
Mama never had a proper
wedding gown. Auntie
used hers to line an infant's coffin.
Mine, inexpensive muslin gone
to wrinkles and strings.

I remember Aunt Fiona
on hands and knees combing
a rag rug for misplaced sequins,
unable to eat until she found them.
At night before retiring she counted,
every spool, darning egg, bone,
wooden and abalone button,
snap, hook, eye, bamboo
embroidery hoop. Not one
particle of dust in her sewing nook,
not one brass clasp out of place.
Baleen shirt and corset stays
neatly stacked in order
of length and width.

Color cards, her passion,
in my dream she lectures on
the science of wedding dress tints:
blue-white dulls the shine
of hair and eye; a touch of cream, artistic.
I raise my hand, ask if cherry
blossoms unbecoming

to an autumn-haired bride?
Here Mother appears and
Auntie's sewing notions turn
to carefully sorted trays of printer's type,
color cards to proof sheets hung
by clothespin on laundry line.
Mama searches newsprint but
cannot find the answer.

Only in my dreams do things square up.

II. HELEN

La Conner, Washington

Yes, like my children,
I've lost considerable
in the recent recession —
but when packing to climb
the Golden Stairs,
cares and sorrows
the only baggage taken.
Tempe and the grandgirls
talk about nothing but
wedding plans and
the pain of cutting back
on trousseaus, common
cambric insertions substituted
for point de Paris lace.
A pampered lot,
the women of today;
given to nerves and tantrums.

I often think of Mother's wedding:
A Kentucky girl, fifteen,
clearing land, burning willow
swags, working ash into soil, then
mixing seed and sand
before sowing. At harvest,
tobacco leaves large as children
pulled and hung upside down,
dried, cured, stitched into "hands."
Late spring brought late floods, hail
ruined what crop remained.
Fleeing to Ohio, her people
surprised to find land so wide
and empty, without church or store.

That summer, when Mother
married Father, not a table
large enough for company until
her brother took the cabin door
from its hinges, seating eight more.
The groom's family brought cured ham,
and to prevent my father from seeing
his bride in her new gingham apron
with two deep pockets before
the preacher arrived, Mother
went to borrow potatoes
from the neighbors, walking
up Pebble Creek lined with rocks
big as haystacks where she feared
mountain cats — which screamed
in the voices of lost children —
behind each one.

The neighbor would not lend
potatoes against next year's crop
as Mother had hoped, but
gave them to her and atop a basket
of brown earth pears, two
brown eggs, which made
Mother weep. For your wedding
cake, the neighbor said.
Walking home through rose briars,
Mother put an egg in each deep
pocket. Potatoes bumping her knees,
one precious shell cracked,
but did not leak. So cake
was made, but where to bake?
All cooking accomplished by fire
and the Dutch oven filled with ham.
The same neighbor had a stove,
which when stoked with rose briar
made a hot oven, and so cake was baked
and Mother prayed she would
not stumble walking home.

When she returned, the feast
table *née* door laid with a new
handwoven tow cloth
as white as salt. Father made
her a black birch chair, stringing
the seat with strips of hide.
They married, their audience
seated on stumps or rails
laid across rocks.

I still have that cloth and chair—
engagement gifts to my grandgirls.

III. Belle

Pendleton, Oregon

You haven't asked about
my wedding or what I wore.
I remember it like yesterday:
tending my brother's sheep
mornings and nights,
trimming hats for Mother
in between times — so I hardly noticed
when the Judge started courting.
No one could fathom why
he'd frequent a millinery shop,
as Pendleton had suffered a fresh
rash of robberies and he'd
more pressing concerns
— which was indeed the case.
The Judge owned a prize ox,
Big Ben, who worked laying
rail line, during which time
he was gored by a wild cow.
The Judge loved that ox
more than life; fret for it
kept him from sleep. When
he came in ordering a poke-
style off-the-face bonnet trimmed
in a cherry wreath and two
rows of tucks encircling the brim,
Mother knew he was courting, she just
didn't know who. Some widow,
she said. And when he begged
me to ride out to his
Broken Spoke Ranch and try
my flaxseed poultice on Old Ben's

wounded foreleg, Mother told me
I couldn't refuse. Days later
the Judge bought a leghorn trimmed
in velvet forget-me-nots
sprayed with June roses and
asked if I'd come out and apply
my turpentine bath
to a calf infested with red mite.

All livestock improved, but I
contracted disfiguring poison oak.
A week later I walked home from
the sunflower-strewn draw where
my brother pastured his ewes, tired
and about out of shoe leather.
My face oozing, my eyes swollen shut;
Mother met me at the door, scolding:
Did I know who'd been waiting
for over an hour?

Of course there was gossip,
talk's sure as taxes.
I'd be the Judge's third wife,
the first two gave out from exhaustion.

Little Peggy Webb, who married
my brother, had lots of stylish clothes;
I had none and asked her for help.
My gown made of pearl pongee,
the skirt a deep kilted flounce.
I had white kid gloves and white
kid slippers. Mother designed
my headgear, and wouldn't speak
to me for weeks when I refused

to wear a veil. She hadn't been
so vexed since the incident
at Webb's Hardware when
I'd minded the store while
the owner went trading:
Patrons on the front porch sitting
on nail kegs watched in-
coming stages, betting which
coach ran ahead or behind.
I knew about Mr. Webb's binoculars
and innocently wagered
five dollars taken from the till.
Of course, I won
and when word got around,
the owner and my mother
were sent for. I'd stolen,
I'd gambled (it was years before
I told how I'd won).
I was twenty-two, unmarried,
and now likely to remain so.
Mother threw up her hands.

My bonnet was straw lined in silk
with white two-inch-wide streamers.
The ceremony festive, though brief—
as I mentioned, our town had suffered
a fresh siege of banditry.
With no room at the jail,
the Judge handcuffed
prisoners to lampposts.
Walking from church
to street, the aroma of urine
stronger than smelling salts.
My new husband resumed

dispensing justice right after
a photographer posed us.

I've never been sorry about the veil.
Looking back, I'd have changed
nothing, except to do it over
as a groom instead of a bride.
I loved to ride horses, and took
to herding cattle like an Indian.
In those days long skirts
hobbled women afoot or astride;
and, in summer, we nearly stewed
under a sweat lodge of hair.
I still have those two
silly cherry wreath and velvet
forget-me-not bonnets — never taken
from their boxes —
trophies,
the last hats I ever trimmed.

IV. HELEN

I guess I'd have to say
electric lights. Yes,
in my opinion that's what
brought on hard times.
I remember one winter
back on Swantown Lane
we hadn't even a kerosene
lamp — saving to buy
the *Gazette* and publish
our own paper. We'd
a tin vessel like a two-
spouted teapot from which

wicks protruded, burning oil
squeezed from the livers
of dogfish — a scent that
tried the stomach! Worse,
the flame tips streamed
smoke, blackening
walls and ceiling. Later,
when my daughter
married and moved
east of the mountains
to an electrified house,
I couldn't believe it —
at dusk, a daylight kitchen.

After strict saving
we acquired our paper
during the Panic of '93.
Unlike Mother, who hid
gold slugs in a haystack,
I kept my little safe in the privy.

Just setting up, children underfoot,
it was the day after Thomas
re-roofed our print shop.
First the air turned heavy as lard,
an eerie darkness descending.
From the ocean sprang wind
too warm for November.
Before our noon meal,
all oil lights lit. Rain fell
in boat holds full, entering
window and door cracks
as if thrown in with a pail.
Suddenly my kitchen felt

like a dry goods crate and
someone was shaking it.
I thought: train derailment,
imagining a black iron
dragon leave its eyesore
of an elevated crossing
and careen toward our little house . . .

Then came the noise of roofs
torn from barn beams,
buildings uprooted;
a tree fell in our front yard,
two in the back. I swear
I saw the footpath creep like a snake.
People outdoors had to lie down
clinging to stumps. From thickly
timbered hills came the shipwreck
thunder of great trees shattering.
Tempe and I fell to the floor,
sobbing, *stop, make it stop*.
Seth and Thomas succeeded
in saving the presses.

Next morning when the rain
let up, everywhere a red snow
of shattered chimneys,
our print shop roof gone.
The breezes of rumor
bit at our ears: children
killed by falling limbs
at the schoolhouse;
Bagpipe Hildebrand blown
end over end, drowned
in his oyster beds. All
telegraph poles downed.

In the parlor, trays of *Gazette* type
headlining "Hurricane" with warnings
of high tide and floods — words
turned to plowshares.
Tempe sketched the deceased,
Seth the destruction
as freshets galloped down
the now naked hills
into a tide of eelgrass.
Floating forest wreckage
broke our windows and
before water covered
our wainscoting, we moved
all presses upstairs.
After greasing the rollers, we
took a pitchfork, turning
sheaves of newsprint
as if drying wheat.

Overnight
we became a paper of record.
With electrified houses and power
printers like you see now,
it wouldn't have happened.
I think that's why I've
always favored a hand press.
The feel of each page —
like a seed sprouting,
leafing out.

After the Great War,
so many easy conveniences.
It got harder to save —
you couldn't cut back

to fish oil lamps. Today
I'd be in a better way
if I'd left my poke
in a haystack or privy
instead of the Mutual. But
a whiff of a ten-candle
light bulb made me never
want to look back
on endless days
of squeezing oil
from the livers of dogfish.

V. SETH

La Conner, Washington

The thought
of a Spokane wedding
brings on migraines and
the memory of my brother-in-law's
sold-off wheat and sugar beet fields:
Acres of little white markers
tagged in red surveyor tape flags,
reminiscent of newly laid out
cemeteries for war dead.

Mother worries about how I'll behave,
though we never speak of it.
At first, years ago, I wasn't sure,
was it she or Tempe?
(Father had an eye
for detail, but not that kind.)
I don't know how
the jug was always found

no matter where I hid it:
In the cow's grain bin,
the potato barrel, the well.
Mother blamed herself.
Age five I got into a tin
of printer's ink which brought
on seizures. The whole
of Swantown Lane
eyed her accusingly —
giving herself to equal suffrage
and anti-liquor leagues
when she ought to be . . .
Suffer the little children,
they quoted: her son crippled,
witless, or poisoned in the way
hatters went mad
from mercury used to felt hats.

I had only wanted to see
what it felt like to be tattooed
black like newsprint.
The story of the suffragette's
baby eating prohibition ink
crackled every telegraph wire.
Mournful eyes fell on Father.
Saloon owners leveled fingers
at Mrs. Hodgson's friends'
husbands as if they were guns
likely to go off. Liquor
the enemy of womanhood?
For weeks her "just desserts" toasted.

Granny's sure cure for seizures,
Blue Ruin and goose broth,

the taste of my childhood.
How long did it take me
to realize they'd started diluting it?
Mother too frugal
to throw away anything;
if I searched the house
thoroughly enough I'd find
the rest, though she was inventive.
A tin marked "Piano Polish"
(we hadn't one), a bottle of Mrs. Wilson's
Women's Complaint Remedy.

After money got scarce
and Father got feeble, falling
on the ice of a newly paved sidewalk,
I brought them here,
little northern seaside village
of dairy fields, peas, mustard
grown for seed.
In summer a tide of yellow
spice rolls below rocky
cypress-covered hillocks
into the gravel-colored sound.
They still publish a weekly,
walk to the mayor's pharmacy,
the bank or what's left of it.

Drops of pepper sauce
must have been Tempe's idea,
a sure cure for what the Great War
and Madeline had done to me.
I never smelled blister gas,
never sat, legs cramped into my gut,
buttocks bones pressing like two

electric cord prongs into the damp
hard floor of a Normandy trench.
Examining shattered London buildings,
my lungs ruined by limestone dust.
Coming home, an inspector's job
in Spokane secured
by Herr brother-in-law.
Madeline's letter
on the kitchen table, no surprise after
I was let go. Instead
of razing leaning brick fortresses,
the city fathers fired me.
Complaints of my moodiness,
of fist-beating-the-desk rages.
Untrue. It was my forehead
banging against varnished oak,
anything to drown out that
never-ceasing day and night rattle-
clank of railroad cars.
And Spokane's smell. Without war
markets, wheat left to rot
by the boxcar load.
Picture square miles of trackage,
engines, stockyards — all idle
while a town the color of rust
and brick dust dreamed
itself Chicago.

Now Tempe sends
magazine clippings: a jockey
(one of theirs before
Howard's bank failed?)
who couldn't live without ale,
never bent his elbow again

after being kicked in the head
by a horse.

I'm careful.
No one would guess.
Sometimes when inspecting
a water tower, a cellar,
I find evidence of membership
in the Secret Order of Silence.

A building inspector knows every trick.

VI. SETH

From Pendleton we used to walk
southwest to a fork in the ravine
road called Pilot Rock, then
due east, left on Yellow Jacket Trail
where stinging insects
fenced off stalks of wild, black-
eyed sunflowers. Why,
every August of my childhood,
did we retrace the journey
of Father's discontent?
Up steep, treeless draws and
rocky buffalo-hump hills covered in
knife-thin grass growing
from a spoonful of topsoil
burned transparent
by a relentless sun;
to a hole dug back
into a gulch with one
sod walled-in window,
a weathered door

with wooden latches,
chimney made of mud
and sticks dug through
the top of the hill.
Sometimes we stayed
at Father's boyhood
sheep camp for a week
where mice ate through sod
followed by snakes. Sleeping
on old mattress tick under
a rough-cut table, we escaped
the hail of spiders as scorpions
fell from the ceiling. Fleas
living in the sparse
grass came through cracks
and we had to take
the mattress tick out, empty it,
wash, fill with fresh straw, scattering
stock salt over the dirt
floor as repellent.

Hot desert nights I lay
sleepless, listening to haunted
coyote hills and
the *click click* of spiders
falling on the tabletop
while Father described (again and
again) the dugout he built
for Mother before they married.

During courtship,
he'd sodded and plastered
front and ceiling, building
a little roof bowed like a boxcar.

All the same, snakes penetrated
during high water, and once
a blue racer burrowed
into the folds of Mother's
only good dress
where it froze to death
and wasn't found
until her wedding day.

Something about
the oppressive smell of cave
dirt and the incessant *tap tap*
of that dream-curdling
arachnid rain made me swear
to build real buildings when
I grew up — structures of wood
and stone and steel reaching
for the firmament, not
something so frighteningly kin
to a grave. The percussive
music of mathematics fueled
those sheep camp nights
where my insomnia took root,
eventually blooming
black-eyed as sunflowers.

VII. HELEN

I would have to say Jell-O.
Some women might say
electric flat irons —
so many in use on the Tuesday
morning my grandgirls were born,
lights shorted out all over town.

I think Mother would have
said: walking into a July
kitchen and seeing
an oven topped by a vase
of garden-fresh zinnias and
a well-cooked ham —
the room air bearable,
those zinnias without
one wilted orange head.
An electric range, that's what
Mother'd have said. And Thomas?
Probably water skimmer-
in-the-sky aeroplanes.
His father swore by the slow
sure rhythm of oxcarts,
the comforting *thwark*
and squeak of harness
hitting singletree. I'll never
forget the happy day my parents
purchased our first horse and
bateau-sized wagon. Buggies?
The trademark of carpetbaggers.
Eventually, when the price
of wool doubled, we did
get a carriage — used Sundays only,
acceleration reserved for arrival
at God's Earthly House. But
then railroads changed Christian
preaching on the evils of speed.
Now, I'm told, from the sky,
with so much rail line trackage
and telephone wire, *terra firma*
looks like the Devil's own crazy quilt.
Never been up in a mechanical kite.

Don't plan to
as it might spoil heaven.

Yes, I'd say Jell-O.
I was a young mother
on Swantown Lane
when a neighbor
brought the first molded
lemon gelatin I'd ever seen
out of her springhouse. A winter
sweet made from August sun,
no need for baking or
the hand-breaking whisk,
just summer-flavored water
chilled in a root cellar.
Electric springhouses and
molded August sunshine?
Diphtheria or the ague,
what fever brought on
such visions?

VIII. DOT

Tacoma, Washington

Can't come to the napkin
embroidery bee Monday night,
I have lodge meeting—
we quilt for newborns, knit
lap robes for invalids.
The reception? I'm making
Wedding-cake-white cake.
Of course baked on the old
woodstove, saves the light bill.

That photo?
My fiftieth birthday party.
Five children still living.
You like my velvet dress?
I'm wearing it to my nieces'
double wedding — the ones
we're embroidering for.
Evening sapphire. My best. My sons
born near our Coeur d'Alene claim,
my baby girl on the tenant farm
where we raised fruit and people paid
us two cents a pound for apples.
Moved across the Cascades
during the Great War and don't miss
rattlesnakes a bit. My husband
built ships here in Tacoma.
He's dead now and I'm sorry
things turned out like they did.
Tried to rent a place in town when
he left. But no one would lease to a man-
less woman with seven kids, so
I sold the cow and yearling calf
for fifty dollars, bought
my house on North Ninth.
Scrubbed floors. Didn't waste
a living thing — saved
apple peelings for making vinegar.
Been cleaning houses since
I turned thirteen and school
ended at grade eight.
Been scrubbing since I was tall
enough to wash cups in a tub
Mama put on a chair seat in front of me —
though washing isn't so bad if

you don't have to haul water.
Which is why
I like my house on North Ninth.
The night of the first Armistice,
my little girl and a friend went out
and didn't come back.
At midnight, I scoured
the neighborhood. At two
I found them swinging in the park!
Nearly fifteen years ago and I'm still
not over the fright. Do you think
those girls would be found alive today?
That one became a ballerina.
My youngest boy drowned
in Spirit Lake. My oldest
died at Verdun. I still
have a letter from his sergeant
saying how stoutly he'd fought.
After I got the others through
high school and myself
a nursing certificate, I bought
a nice dress. Elected two terms
as Worthy Grand Matron,
Rebecca Lodge Number 6, and
wanted to look the part. My last
ten dollars, an extravagance. But
I couldn't resist a skirt
the color of the sky that night
I found my daughter safe —
even if it has the plaits and sweep
of a before-the-war gown.
I got double S & H green stamps
when I bought it and have
worn it to every birthday,
wedding, and funeral since.

IX. Thomas

La Conner, Washington

Added to this week's Gazette,
extra leaves inked with lists
of foreclosures like obituaries
during polio season.
My daughter turns to
Engagement Announcements,
pitying one of the grandgirls'
bridesmaids forced to substitute
lard for butter on bread.

As a child, I knew neither and
remember asking Mother, What
made the coffee taste odd?
— brewed from never-before-tasted
real beans, not roasted barley.
I hated its bitterness,
the flavor of maggot.
Mother said she could fix that,
adding Indian salt which I'd never
eaten but loved and wanted
Mrs. Columbia Joe to bring
more of until I discovered bags
of it at the trading post
marked "Sugar."

My daughter says if she ever
found herself in a kitchen
without necessities, she'd rather
drink rat poison than spend
her day boiling and straining
cantaloupe the way we did

when sugar was luxury
not staple. Flour, I tell her,
flour, the hardest thing
to do without.

One autumn Father and I flailed
our wheat by hand,
cleaning with wind power,
then ground kernels to dust
in a coffee mill — days
to make a loaf of bread.
Come baking time, we'd been
too busy to tend fire and since
we'd no matches, had to borrow
coals from a neighbor
which was how I met my wife
whose father had plenty and who
gave me a job tending sheep,
paying in salt and a new
gear for our grinder.

Lonely days of chasing ewes
through buckthorn and sage,
I dreamed a string of windmills
and millponds, the never-ceasing
desert blow rolling down
the gorge trained to raise water
Columbia River to ridge
which wasn't practical though
we pumped onto our flatlands
and grew more wheat;
engines fueled by driftwood —
this before trees cut down
to feed cinder-spewing
steamboat smokestacks.

Today Roosevelt has more
grandiose schemes:
a million-dollar, fifty-story
dam at Coulee City,
built by cattlecar loads
of Spokane's unshaven
slouch-capped men, paid
by government relief.
My son fans himself
with a newspaper, tired
of hearing how his granddad
built a sod house for only
ten dollars and borrowed team,
trading a lend of his lathe
for labor.

Never saw a treasury note
until Father sold his span of oxen.
When stockmen and passersby
stopped for a night at our soddie,
they rarely paid with a long and short
or single two-bit coin, but
a cabbage, a pair of candles, once
a scrap of muslin which Mother
unraveled and twisted into thread.
I try to tell my children and grandgirls,
the terrible difference between
these hard times and my boyhood is

though we had nothing,
we all had nothing alike.

X. BELLE

Six months after my wedding,
Mother called me back to her shop
to trim a hat for a woman
because she was afraid
to do it and since I was
the Judge's wife, no
one would criticize.
No relief agencies then,
neighbor looked after neighbor
more than they do today.
There'd been a terrible
train derailment near Butter Creek
and our county commissioners
gave one new widow a lump sum
of a hundred dollars. She took
a steamboat to Portland,
bought herself the nicest sea
green cashmere tea costume
Umatilla had ever seen, then
sent to Paris for a Bulgarian lamb
driving coat and Common Sense
opera slippers to match. Finally
she went to Mother's hat shop
for Ivanhoe-style headgear.
Which is where I was called in,
as everyone chided
the widow's extravagance.
Two months later, tongues
stopped wagging when she married
the L. P. & M. ticket agent and was
thereafter considered a woman
of judgment. Best
investment ever made,
all commissioners agreed. But

a shopping trip downriver
and a well-trimmed hat aren't
going to fix all the soup kitchens
and bread lines of today. Neither
is the Red Cross nor
Methodist Church Relief.
On the sidewalk in front
of my house, countless
chalk lines, code to so many
derailed men that
a knock on my door
will bring a scrap of cheese
and ham in exchange
for raking leaves.
My neighbors' tongues chide
Mr. Roosevelt's extravagance, but
not one chalk line on the sidewalk
in front of the brass knockers
on their doors.

XI. LOTTIE WICKE

Spokane, Washington

I remember it clearly,
the first time the voice spoke,
commanding: Lottie,
pen and paper, not
thread and thimble.
Odd, because bridal patterns
on my mind for weeks.

It happened the day Father
walked into the gambrel-

roofed foaling barn
to check the suckling gray
and investigate the fuss
a pigeon brought on.
I'd just asked Trudy: Would white
velvet shoulder capes add
height to our gowns?
Father thought my fiancé's
fingers too pale, handshake
limp as an eel.
I watched as he worked
his palms over the foal,
withers to rump, as if searching
for something lost.

White watered satin, Trudy said,
with knife-pleated puffs at the neck.
What did I think? I wondered
about dainty pigeons
embroidered on our veils and
prayed for a sign.

After the suckling colt,
whom Trudy named Grayling,
got kicked in the jaw
by his racehorse dam — last
descendant of famed Chehalis —
Father's mood turned a darker hue.
He proclaimed that Trudy's fiancé
shuffled in a saunter instead
of a walk. Their major sin: Neither
son-in-law-to-be knew a thing
about banking or bloodlines.

As Father's prize foal recuperated
at Old Bess's side, the nurse mare
eyed her charge like a green fly,
glancing at her flanks while
he sucked, as if something
were amiss with the breeching
of her long-ago harness.

Trudy, with her gift
for doctoring beasties,
had taken on foal's care
getting engaged to the new
veterinary surgeon.
Five times a day we fed
Grayling cracked corn soaked
in honeycomb from
a bear tree Drover found
near Hangman Creek. Gruel
slid from the lips of foal's
broken, wired-together mouth,
what milk teeth remained hitting
wrong in a *clap-clap* as he ate.
Trudy's fiancé wanted
to give up farm husbandry
and take on the study of molds.
My intended sold wireless
receivers and dreamed of moving
to London where they broadcast
using a new kind of signal.

Trudy told Father: Grayling
needed companionship as Old Bess
never cavorted with her charge,
would not wheel, rear, run

the fenceline, but remained planted,
moving slow as glaciermelt from purple
clover to clover; the nurse mare snaking
her neck at our Derby hopeful,
ears pinned in annoyance.

Pigeons marry for life, so
we didn't know why a lone bird
came to roost in the barn eaves.
The same color as Grayling, which
is what gave me the idea. Father
ordered Drover: Shoot it, but
I begged no, moving the nest
to Old Bess's stall where Pij
pecked at the manger floor,
ate honeyed corn fallen
from Grayling's mouth as the colt's
muzzle butted Pij in play.

That morning at breakfast,
Father had allowed that
our suckling improved,
his first smile in weeks—
as if in fixing the foal, he could
mend the First National,
restore Spokane streets
to the laughter-filled air
of five years ago.

Was it Pij's fog-colored feathers
and foal's mousy coat
which bound them?
Foal turned out to paddock,
Pij followed, perched on a gate post.

Then — I could not believe
my eyes — Pij flew the fenceline,
Grayling galloping after
up and back, up and . . .
Old Bess's head turned,
mirrored our stunned stare
at bird exercising race colt:
For a moment I forgot
gored skirts and champagne silk.
Into the corner, across the diagonal,
around the far turn, down the home
stretch, faster, fast enough to
out-fly a bird to the hollowed
log water-trough-of-a-finish line.

That was the first time
I heard the voice command:
Lottie, pen and paper, not
thimble and muslin.

XII. HELEN

My daughter asks,
What should they sing?
Lately at sunset, an old
Overland tune — lullaby
of my cradle days — skips
inside my head:

*From this Valley
they say you are leaving . . .*

Yes, I expect
one night soon Somnus

will bear me past
the land of Nod to the blue
lily-studded Hills
of Toil-and-Spin Not.
My daughter asks again,
What, what song?

We will miss your bright eyes
and sweet smile . . .

Wedding or funeral?
I've forgotten. What I'd like
to hear one more time

They say you are taking the sunshine . . .

is Mother as she sat
beside the pink rockrose
in our Umatilla garden
humming in a minor key.

That brightened our pathway awhile . . .

Behind her, silhouette of the big-
bellied Horse Heaven Hills and
a watermelon sunset spreading
across a red river of the sky.
On either side, two split
halves of a broken grindstone —
my brothers' grave markers.

Do not hasten to bid me adieu . . .

If I could hear her voice
clear and high as glass

bells one last . . . I see
her so plainly — hands

. . . the one who loved you so true . . .

strong as willow trunks
stretching out to me:

"*Come sit*, Helen,
while I sing to Buck and Chip."

And before the sky turns
to the shivery violet
velvet color of sage flowers,
the voices of our a cappella

Come sit by my side
if you love me . . .

drift across treeless
sheep-spotted hills.